# SECRETS

*of the*

# KINGDOM
# ECONOMY

# SECRETS
*of the*
# KINGDOM ECONOMY

*How You Can Flourish
in God's Economy*

## PAUL L. CUNY

Previously published as *Secrets of the Kingdom Economy* by Paul L. Cuny Second Printing 2008 ISBN: 978-0-9796916-0-7 by Bethany Press.

DESTINY IMAGE₀ PUBLISHERS, INC.

P.O. Box 310, Shippensburg, PA 17257-0310

*"Speaking to the Purposes of God for This Generation and for the Generations to Come."*

This book and all other Destiny Image, Revival Press, MercyPlace, Fresh Bread, Destiny Image Fiction, and Treasure House books are available at Christian bookstores and distributors worldwide.

For a U.S. bookstore nearest you, call 1-800-722-6774.

For more information on foreign distributors, call 717-532-3040.

Reach us on the Internet: www.destinyimage.com.

ISBN 13 Trade Paper: 978-0-7684-3707-2

ISBN 13 Hard Copy: 978-0-7684-3708-9

ISBN 13 Large Print: 978-0-7684-3709-6

ISBN 13 E-book: 978-0-7684-9018-3

For Worldwide Distribution, Printed in the U.S.A.

1 2 3 4 5 6 7 8 9 10 / 15 14 13 12 11

# *Acknowledgments*

My deepest gratitude goes to my friend, my confidante, and my wife, Gerri, for her partnership, insight, and wisdom in our life together and in this project. I discovered once again your God-given drive for excellence.

I want to express my sincerest appreciation to my friend Rob Sanders, who was consistent with his encouragement, full of godly insight, perceptive in his theological review, and generous with his precious time and prayers.

My heartfelt thanks also goes to my covenant friends: Jim Young, Paul Wilbur, Ben Goldsmith, Paul Zink, and Paul Williams. You taught me that to maintain a big vision, I must associate with people who have the same heart and a similar vision. You brothers recognized the purpose of God in me and helped me begin the journey toward fulfilling it. Thank you for your friendship, for believing in me all these years, and for making room for me in your lives.

My sincere gratitude goes to Andres Marquez, who is a trusted friend, a lover of God and people, full of wisdom and counsel, and tireless with his prayers and efforts for the Spanish-speaking world.

I am grateful for Jan Christie, a friend, counselor, and intercessor for many leaders in the marketplace movement. We are all thankful for the endless hours you spend in prayer over our lives and unique callings, and for your influence in Heaven on our behalf.

I want to thank Dan Duke for helping me discover the reality of Jesus Christ.

*Endorsements*

Paul Cuny's book on God's Kingdom Economy is one of the best books ever for workplace leaders. Every working Christian should read this book. It has fresh insights and a depth that you will not find in other marketplace books. Well done, Paul!

Os Hillman
President, Marketplace Leaders
Author of *The 9 to 5 Window*
and *TGIF Today God Is First*

To some, the whole concept of a ministry in what is known as the "marketplace" is a very foreign idea, but to Paul Cuny it is a life calling. You will find that calling and vision in the pages of this book along with a passion and wisdom for changing the economies of nations. You might be asking yourself, "Is this just another grandiose title with no substance to fill in the blanks?" I can assure you that revelation and impartation await you within the covers of this book.

Paul Cuny is a board member and a trusted personal friend and co-laborer who has stood beside me in ministry on several continents and before princes. He is a mature man of God who has lived the covenant and proven himself as a faithful man, as well as a gifted man. You will be blessed and challenged as you read these words that come from a vessel that has been broken and fashioned by the hands of the Master Potter.

Paul Wilbur
President, Paul Wilbur Ministries
Author of *Order in the Courts*


It has been a privilege to minister with Paul in a number of nations, from Central America to Africa. *Secrets of the Kingdom Economy* reflects his life and passion for the presence of God. In my opinion, the heart of his book is the statement that "Activity will never produce My presence. My presence will always produce focused, productive activity." Paul lives what he is teaching. His insights about the Kingdom Economy are unique and will be a blessing to all who put them into practice. The principles in this book apply to all walks of life—not just the marketplace! I have been challenged by Paul's life and teaching to know the Lord more intimately. I believe all who read this book will experience the same challenge!

Paul Williams, MD
President, International HealthCare Network
Author of *When All Plans Fail*

*Secrets of the Kingdom Economy* is a download from Heaven for our times. In a world where people are confused and struggling about their real purpose and calling in life, this book is a unique resource that will enable them to finally see their destiny clearly. So many people want to serve God and yet are confused about whether to serve as a pastor or in business, education, or government. This book will liberate them.

Many others have struggled for years with handling money. The biblical principles in this book, if followed, will most certainly yield abundant fruit in the life of the believer. Paul did not get these principles by reading them in someone else's book—he received them from God as he walked them out.

Jim Young
Land Developer


Today's world is broken and fragmented in key settings such as family, business, community, government, media, religion, and education. This status quo urges a shift in the way we as leaders are expected to respond, think, plan, behave, make decisions, and resolve conflicts.

I had the privilege of serving as an interpreter to Paul Cuny in conferences held before several hundred leaders in Latin America. After that experience, and our special times of prayer, discussion, and analysis of the marketplace and the secrets of the Kingdom Economy, I can say that Paul has a special calling in his life which he embraces and performs with a passion. Paul has captured, in this book, the essence of what I have found is the heart of transforming leadership in any work or ministerial setting. Paul challenges the reader with insightful questions at the end of each chapter as a means of application of the content.

Paul Cuny not only teaches these principles to leaders worldwide, but most exciting to me, he lives by these principles himself as a husband, father, and professional. *Secrets of the Kingdom Economy* is without a doubt soon to become a consulting manual among leaders who are willing to transform society.

Dr. DSL Alejandro Amaya
Psychologist and Consultant

It is a rare occasion when you find someone who has revelation knowledge coupled with strong scriptural backing. In the case of Paul Cuny and his teaching on the Kingdom Economy, he has been given the gift to impart this knowledge to the Body of Christ. As you read through the insights that God has given through him, open your heart and let your mind be transformed by his words. It is time for us to operate in Kingdom realities in every aspect of our life. Paul truly is a gift that has come into the Kingdom for such a time as this.

Bishop Paul D. Zink
Senior Pastor, New Life Christian Fellowship
Jacksonville, Florida

*Secrets of the Kingdom Economy* teaches us the key principles that we need to strengthen our understanding and the practical steps that we need to take in order to be a servant of God in the Kingdom Economy. Quoting Paul, "The trade routes of Kingdom Economy must be pure" and "leaders must go outside of the camp." This book provides excellent teaching material for all of us who are called to serve God at our workplace. It gives a different perspective and strength to continue to promote "Faith at Work."

Pierre Yourougou, PhD
Associate Professor of Finance and Kiebach Fellow,
Syracuse University
Former Senior Officer of the World Bank

Paul L. Cuny is a rare emerging leader in the Body of Christ today. Paul has a unique "diffusing grace" in his speaking and writing: a divine anointing to open the hearts and minds of workplace believers and communicate God's heart to His people, not only with relevant Kingdom economic principles, but also with the impartation of the Holy Spirit. *Secrets of the Kingdom Economy* is a must-read for every pastor and workplace believer.

Rev. Dr. Michael F. Bartolomeo Sr.
Senior Pastor, Church for the Harvest
Alexandria, Minnesota

Jesus said as part of the Lord's Prayer, *"As it is in heaven so shall it be on earth." Secrets of the Kingdom Economy* is a release of Heaven into the Kingdom Economy on Earth, and it will produce much fruit when the principles contained in its pages are applied. Every Christian businessperson should use this book as their company manual. Paul Cuny also brings God's heart for business as a ministry into perspective. This book will bring release to many who are called to be marketplace entrepreneurs and Kingdom builders.

Pastor Ian Johnson
His Amazing Glory Ministries
Auckland, New Zealand
Author of *Glory to Glory*

*Secrets of the Kingdom Economy* is the book the Body of Christ around the world has been waiting for!

Rev. Edward Dawkins, Attorney at Law
ThM, Dallas Theological Seminary

*Secrets of the Kingdom Economy* is a riveting read. It is changing my life. Paul Cuny expounds biblical "secrets" that challenge a response and spur one to action. As a businessman, much of my time is spent planning, strategizing, connecting, and coordinating. But God, who is omnipotent and omniscient, desires us to "connect" with Him because He has "*The* Plan." This book has sharpened my sense of mission in my business. It is a business plan based on the Bible.

Ong Siow Aik
Founder and Managing Director
OSA Industries Group of Companies
Singapore

# Table of Contents

# *Foreword*

*Secrets of the Kingdom Economy* by Paul Cuny is an important book. To begin with, it is born out of years of leading the Christian life through worship, prayer, study, running a business, consulting, and praying with marketplace and political leaders around the world. Second, this book teaches Kingdom principles and how to apply them, especially in the marketplace and in government. If the ideas in this book are implemented, they will change the politics and economies of nations.

Although this book was primarily written for the people of God, it has immediate relevance for all people of goodwill who seek to transform the economies of their nations, especially in the developing world. Paul Cuny believes that in order for this to happen, pastors, marketplace leaders, and government leaders must work together to establish the good government and just economies that bless a nation's people.

This book will bless anyone who reads it with an open heart, but it is especially relevant to marketplace and political leaders. It will enable them to exercise the kind of godly leadership that transforms businesses, economies, and political and social institutions. Also, I recommend that pastors teach the principles of this book to their congregations. This will allow God to call forth Kingdom leaders for government, business, labor, and finance. Further, being a Kingdom leader can be difficult. Pastoral support, encouragement, intercession, and accountability are crucial. Paul Cuny's book will enable pastors to support Kingdom leaders in their vital work. I cannot recommend it too highly.

Finally, as a pastor of many years, and as one who has lived and worked among the poor in developing countries that are desperately in need of political and economic justice and mercy, I give *Secrets of the Kingdom Economy* my best and most heartfelt recommendation.

Rev. Robert J. Sanders, PhD
Author of *Face to Face*
www.rsanders.org

# Introduction

I have had the privilege of bringing the message of the Kingdom to marketplace believers in many nations around the world. There seems to be an unprecedented hunger in every nation among believers in the marketplace who are no longer content to stay in the shadows of mediocrity. They are bold and pressing for the Kingdom to come in the marketplace. This generation is represented by men and women in all nations who are developing a decidedly Kingdom worldview.

You and I are living in the days of the Kingdom that Jesus spoke about when He taught us to pray by saying *"Thy kingdom come! Thy will be done..."* (Matt. 6:10 KJV). The Kingdom is here. If we learn to function by the principles of that Kingdom in our day-to-day lives, we will function on a higher level of anointing and productivity.

Living in this Kingdom means living by the *Secrets of the Kingdom Economy.*

However, the Kingdom Economy is not a new teaching on biblical economics. It was part of the plan God gave Moses for the nation of Israel. Today, instead of application to one nation and one people, we will see the Kingdom Economy established worldwide. We are experiencing a restoration of God's system of economics to the marketplace.

For many of us, the understanding of this economy has been summed up in four words: "giving tithes and offerings." These four words do represent an essential component, but the Kingdom Economy is vast in scope and broad in application to our day-to-day lives. His economic system must be established in the marketplace to bring about the Kingdom Jesus spoke about.

Though we live in a very different day from Isaac, Moses, or Amos, the principles by which God's economy functions have remained practical and effective because they have His authorization. God is not technologically challenged or out of date. In fact, He told the prophet Daniel almost 500 years before the birth of Jesus about the technology of our day (see Dan. 12:4). God had a complete understanding of the Internet before Adam first walked this earth! He doesn't have to revise His strategic plan to an updated version—He is current and forward-thinking in His plan for humankind.

A number of years ago, during an early morning time of prayer, the Lord spoke to my spirit, "I am preparing to make My economic system the dominant system on the earth, and you are to teach My people how to live in My economic system."

My first response was, "Lord, if I am to teach Your people, You must first teach me!" In the months and years that followed, I received a biblical education by the Holy Spirit that continues even today. I discovered that the Scripture is filled with economic principles that are timeless in their application and supernatural in their results.

Most of my Christian life, I have been an entrepreneur and business owner with a heart for ministry to people. I've traveled around the world as one of God's ambassadors to the marketplace. My background as a businessman has given me a unique platform to speak to God's people. Discovering biblical principles for business and government in the Kingdom Economy has enabled me to find God's sovereign hand in unlikely situations. It is my desire to share with you what I have been given so that you may flourish. God has established these principles in my own life and in the lives of the people represented in this book.

As you read, it will become clear to you that there are two distinctly separate kingdoms with their respective economic systems. These two economic systems function simultaneously in our world, and they are integral parts of their respective kingdoms. Just as the kingdoms are in direct conflict with one another, so these economic systems are also in opposition because of conflicting objectives, goals, and results in the lives of the participants.

You will discover that the atmosphere of the Kingdom of God is one of hope and freedom. God's desire is to move us to the place where we function in our gifts. When this happens, He can bring about tangible results in our daily lives. The Kingdom has an atmosphere of service, but never bondage. The wonderful thing about this Kingdom is that it includes a place for the admiral and the seaman, the preacher and the painter, the missionary, the homemaker, and the businessman. In this Kingdom it is not our occupation that God places the highest value on, but the character within us.

As you read this book, you may find that some of these principles are already operational in your life. Others will be new to you. All of them will impact your life during the workweek, as they are practical in their daily application. I'm certain you will be challenged to draw closer to God, but probably for reasons different from what you may think.

It is my hope that as you read this book, you will discover the true meaning of the Kingdom Economy. God's economy is a supernatural one that will enable you to become His representative in the marketplace. You are going to find that God wants a partnership with you, so He will be able to say, *"...you will again distinguish between the righteous and the wicked, between one who serves God and one who does not serve Him"* (Mal. 3:18).

# CHAPTER 1

## The Kingdom of God
## Requires Living
## by Kingdom Economics

*For the land, into which you are entering to possess it, is not like the land of Egypt from which you came, where you used to sow your seed and water it with your foot like a vegetable garden. But the land into which you are about to cross to possess it, a land of hills and valleys, drinks water from the rain of heaven, a land for which the LORD your God cares; the eyes of the LORD your God are always on it, from the beginning even to the end of the year. It shall come about, if you listen obediently to My commandments which I am commanding you today, to love the LORD your God and to serve Him with all your heart and all your soul, that He will give the rain for your land in its season, the early and late rain, that you may gather in your grain and your new wine and your oil. He will give grass in your fields for your cattle, and you will eat and be satisfied* (Deuteronomy 11:10-15).

These powerful verses describe the beginnings of an entirely new culture for God's people. They were finally going to the land that was promised after 400 years of bondage in Egypt. They were being led by the manifest presence of God (the pillar of cloud and pillar of fire), to a land He had reserved for His people. In fact, a heathen people were already tilling their land, building their cities, and cultivating their vineyards. No start-up capital was necessary for their small businesses in this new land. Their agricultural businesses were waiting for them.

What is unique about this moment in history is that the Lord was also promising His people an unprecedented level of involvement in the economics of this nation. These verses represent the beginning of a second economic system. Before this moment, God's economic blessing was given to individuals. Now, for the first time, we see God's economic system being established on a national scale. We are living in the days when God is restoring His system of economics to the marketplace in every nation on earth. It is a system that will enable families, businesses, governments, and nations to flourish because of God's unprecedented involvement in all aspects of culture.

## ATTENTION TO DETAILS

In the preceding verses in the Book of Deuteronomy, Moses said the Lord was sending them to *"...a land for* *which the L*ORD *your God cares; the eyes of the L*ORD *your God are always on it, from the beginning even to the end of the year."* In this new land, God would personally attend to one of the most important elements of agriculture: watering the crops. He was not going to give indiscriminate rainfall but targeted, carefully timed rainfall: the former rain, which gives the germination stage of agriculture the necessary boost, and the latter rain, which is necessary for the crops to reach full potential.

He said He would even give grass for the cattle to eat. How could it be that the Lord actually watched over these fields, herds, and vineyards? Why would He attend to every detail necessary for the economic success of an entire nation of people? Why would God care whether these businesses succeeded? This must have been an inconceivable paradigm shift to a people who for almost 400 years had been the primary labor force for one of the most powerful nations on earth. God was establishing a new economic system called the Kingdom Economy.

## RESTORATION OF THE PARTNERSHIP

Today, marketplace people around the world have a growing awareness of this same economic system— the Kingdom Economy. Living productively in this new economic system required a change of thinking for the people of Israel in the days of the Exodus. God's engagement in their economy shaped their success, not just their human effort and ingenuity. They were required to till and cultivate the ground and plant and harvest the crops, but their labor was in partnership with God. To live productively in this Kingdom Economy today requires a change of thinking on our part as well.

In our day, we are seeing a restoration of these principles taking place. The principles of God's economic system have always been there. However, because we now live in the Kingdom age, these principles are being restored. It is important to understand that the message of the Kingdom Economy is not a new teaching that is sweeping the earth; it is not a new way of conducting business; it is not a matter of sanitizing what exists. This is a restoration of the principles of God's Kingdom Economy to the marketplace.

## Two Kingdoms

Jesus went about preaching the gospel of the Kingdom everywhere He went. Jesus made over 150 references to the "Kingdom" in the New Testament. When He taught us how to pray, He included the phrase *"…Thy kingdom come…"* (see Matt. 6:10; Luke 11:2 KJV). He went about preaching the gospel of the Kingdom. In Matthew 6, He told us to seek the Kingdom first (see Matt. 6:33). The topic of "the Kingdom" was mentioned throughout His parables. Yet it is also clear that Jesus recognized another kingdom, and that these two kingdoms are in conflict with one another.

Jesus successfully endured temptation from the devil in Matthew 4:8-9:

> *Again, the devil took Him to a very high mountain and showed Him all the kingdoms of the world and their*

*glory; and he said to Him, "All these things I will give You, if You fall down and worship me."*

Is satan able to give these kingdoms of the world to Jesus? In John 12:31, Jesus referred to satan as *"the ruler of this world."* In Second Corinthians 4:4, the apostle Paul referred to him as *"the god of this world."* The Greek for *world* is *kosmou,* derived from the word *kosmos,* which means "order, arrangement, ornament, adornment."[1] The things of this world have a system or an order to them.

What are these two opposing "kingdoms"? And what does all this have to do with economics?

## Two Worldviews in Conflict

First, we must realize that these two "kingdoms," the Kingdom of God that Jesus spoke about and the kingdom of this world, are essentially two completely different realities. Each reality is expressed in our lives by our worldview. Our worldview determines our behavior, not only in the marketplace but in our approach to life itself. Just as these kingdoms are in conflict with one another, so these worldviews are also in conflict. For example, one worldview may be represented in business by a drive for success at any cost, corruption, manipulation of clients, greed, selfish ambitions, self-promotion, and self-interest as the top priorities in dealings with others.

We may experience the worldview of the Kingdom through integrity in business dealings, generosity, loyalty, faithfulness, honoring our commitments even when it costs us, and loving and blessing those who use us and seek to destroy us. Our behavior always exposes the worldview of our kingdom. These kingdoms are direct opposites in their very nature.

## GOALS AND OBJECTIVES

These worldviews are completely different because their goals and objectives are different. One worldview is godless and will place man and his achievements at the center of worship (though it will never be defined as worship). The other is a theocracy with God as the sovereign Ruler. One is the system of the world and the other is the Kingdom of God that Jesus spoke about. According to the Book of Revelation, one system will eventually lead to the coming of the antichrist. The second will lead us to the coming of the Messiah. Both worldviews are realities. Both operate simultaneously in the world. It is up to us to choose which reality we will live in.

If we live in the Kingdom of God, then we must come under His Lordship and operate by His principles as they are laid out for us in Scripture.

What does all this have to do with economics? It is impossible to be a participant in either of these kingdoms, with their respective worldviews, without living by the system of economics required by those kingdoms. Just as the Kingdom of God and the kingdoms of this world are polar opposites, so these economic systems are also polar opposites in their objectives, methods of operation, and impacts on the lives of individual participants. Each economic system produces fruit in our lives that reflects the nature of the author of the system.

Dr. Francis A. Schaeffer in his book *A Christian Manifesto* says it this way:

These two world views stand as totals in complete antithesis to each other in content and also in their natural results—including sociological and governmental results, and specifically including law.[2]

What was taking place in Deuteronomy 11:10-15 with the people of Israel was a precursor to what is taking place in our world today. We are living in a time when the principles of the Kingdom are being established. God wants His people to be distinguished today by their integrity, humility, and power. There is no question that His people, whether in Africa, South America, the Far East, or Europe, can operate by the same standards of the Kingdom Economy and they will produce consistent results.

He causes us to prosper, not for our sake, but for the sake of His Kingdom. Deuteronomy 8:18 says:

*But you shall remember the Lord your God, for it is He who is giving you power to make wealth, that He may confirm His covenant which He swore to your fathers, as it is this day.*

Again, Francis Schaeffer says:

It is not that these two world views are different only in how they understand the nature of reality and existence. They also inevitably produce totally different results. The operative word here is *inevitably*. It is not just that they happen to bring forth different results, but it is absolutely *inevitable* that they will bring forth different results.[3]

These two systems differ from one another in practical, tangible ways. When we understand how they differ, we will be better able to live in the Economy of the Kingdom. We will discuss some of the specifics of these systems in subsequent chapters.

## THE KINGDOM ECONOMY

Many of us are aware of the Kingdom Economy. We have adopted many of its principles in our business lives, but our understanding is limited. Several years ago, during one of my early morning times of prayer, the Lord said to me, "I am preparing to make My economic system the dominant economic system in the earth." Over the succeeding months and years, as a result of the Lord opening the "eyes of my understanding" about these things, my thinking was transformed. This preparation for the dominance of the Kingdom Economy is happening today. If the Lord is planning to make this Kingdom Economy the dominant economy on the earth, then we need a deeper understanding.

What are the characteristics of these two economic systems? How do we position ourselves for the level of engagement the Lord promised in the text in Deuteronomy? How can we succeed in this Kingdom Economy? In order to answer these questions we must look at some characteristics of each system.

## CONFIDENCE IN GOD OR MAMMON

Jesus said in Luke 16:13:

*No servant can serve two masters; for either he will hate the one and love the other, or else he will be loyal to the one and despise the other. You cannot serve God and mammon* (NKJV).

Jesus tells us here that service is a requirement for both masters. He says that it is impossible to serve God and serve mammon. Jesus is saying here that dual service is impossible; it cannot be done. You either have to serve one or the other, but you can't serve both. The reason is they are in direct opposition to one another. When we come to the Father, we freely choose to serve Him as a bondservant (a willing servant of a benevolent Master). This is the central theme to the Kingdom Economy. On the other hand, if we choose to serve mammon we choose slavery and bondage. Mammon is a ruthless taskmaster.

Jesus is also speaking about confidence here. When we serve the Lord, we are confident in Him for provision, health, our future, our family, etc. We are confident He will provide for us because His name is Jehovah Jireh (our Provider). In Scripture the many names of God reflect His nature. He does not relinquish this role as Provider in our lives to our employers, our inheritance, our businesses, or our wealth.

No matter what difficulty you are in, He is more than enough. No matter what your finances look like, He will provide. You have ample resource because He is Provider for His people. If you are an entrepreneur in need of business, trust Him for provision. If you are a government leader running for elective office, trust in Him for votes. If you are leader of a large corporation, be confident in Him for wisdom to lead. In the Kingdom Economy our confidence is in Him and Him alone.

## MAMMON

Mammon is one of the foundations of the worldly economy. In Luke 16, Jesus must have carefully chosen the Aramaic term *mammon* to illustrate a profound truth. What exactly is mammon? The word *mammon* is often mistakenly interpreted as "money." Mammon means "confidence in wealth or power; that which is to be trusted."

The original Aramaic word means "avarice (or greed) deified."[4] Mammon is a principality, a demonic force. Not only can people be influenced by this demonic force, but entire nations are ruled by this demonic principality. Since mammon is demonic, it demands people's confidence and service. Mammon is a spirit of greed and avarice that drives the world's system. In this system money, power, or wealth is the ultimate goal.

However, this system never brings fulfillment or satisfaction because you will never have enough. Mammon will always drive you to get more and won't let you enjoy what you have. Mammon promotes a misplaced confidence. It wants you to place your confidence in anything but God. Jesus tells us your confidence is either in mammon or God, but it is an impossibility to have confidence in both.

## WE ARE MISFITS!

In many nations, believers in the marketplace feel like misfits. They struggle and wonder, *Is God calling me into the professional ministry?* I have asked myself that question many times and so do most serious believers who work in the marketplace. He may be calling you to the professional ministry, however His calling does not come by default, because you are uncomfortable or have failed in the marketplace.

Here is the good news: you are never going to fit in the world's system. You are supposed to be uncomfortable because you were made to operate in the Kingdom. Kingdom economic principles, when applied with the correct motives, will always dominate the worldly system because they are supernatural and authorized by the God of the universe. Your access to God's wisdom can cause you to stand out from your peers. You can know things others can't know because your Comforter, the Holy Spirit, speaks and guides. Promotion will come when it may not make sense to others because you walk with the favor of God.

## THE DOMINANT ECONOMY

We live in distressing yet exciting times. It is incumbent upon us, as leaders in the marketplace, to understand the principles of this Kingdom not only for ourselves, but so that we can train and mentor the next generation. I have seen a passion in the next generation to know the ways of God in the marketplace. I have also heard this same generation say, "We need fathers to teach us the ways of God in business!" Oh Lord, give them the fathers, so we may say as Moses said, *"…let me know Your ways that I may know You, so that I may find favor in Your sight"* (Exod. 33:13).

ENDNOTES

1. W.E. Vine, An Expository Dictionary of New Testament Words (Nashville, TN: Royal Publishers, 1939), 1245.

2. Dr. Francis A. Schaeffer, *A Christian Manifesto* (Westchester, IL: Crossway Books, 1981), 18.

3. Schaeffer, 18.

4. James Strong, STD, LLD, *A Concise Dictionary of the Words in the Greek Testament* (Nashville, TN: Abington, 1890), 46.

# CHAPTER 1

## *Questions for Consideration*

1. Have you ever considered that God wants to be actively involved in the work you perform on a daily basis?

_____

_____

_____

_____

_____

2. Have you ever asked Him for His active participation in your work life?

_____

_____

_____

_____

_____

_____

_____

3. Which economic system, as described in this
   chapter, do you find yourself participating in?

_____

_____

_____

_____

_____

_____

_____

4. Jesus described a confidence in God or a confidence in mammon. Where is your confidence
   for your daily life and your future? Is it in your
   money, your family, your knowledge, and your
   abilities, or is it in your God?

_____

_____

_____

_____

_____

_____

_____

5. Have you ever felt like you did not fit in the work environment you were in?

_____

_____

_____

_____

_____

_____

_____

_____

# CHAPTER 2

## The Presence of God
## Is Our Mark of Distinction

*For how then can it be known that I have found favor in Your sight, I and Your people? Is it not by Your going with us, so that we, I and Your people, may be distinguished from all the other people who are upon the face of the earth?* (Exodus 33:16)

Moses was having one of his personal, face-to-face conversations with God. His comments were profound, and they are just as relevant today as when they were first spoken. Moses was saying that by the presence of God and by His personal involvement in the details of the culture of this new nation of people, they would be distinguished from all other people on the earth. In Moses' day, all other nations served heathen gods. There had to be something that would differentiate God's people from everyone else.

Through the Torah (the Law), God began to give Moses and His people the requirements to create an atmosphere for His presence to dwell in. God promised that not only would His presence dwell in the Tabernacle, but in their farms, their businesses, their homes, their government, and in every aspect of the culture of this new nation.

The Lord was speaking to a people who would form a nation composed of farmers and herdsmen, as most nations at that time had agrarian economies. He told Moses that when His people lived by the guidelines of the Torah, their obedience would bring His presence. His presence would produce tangible benefits to the economics of the individual, but also to the nation's economy as a whole. The presence of God was the mark of distinction.

In Deuteronomy 11, the Lord said some astounding things to Moses about His intention for this new nation. God said He would bring about tangible benefits to this agrarian economy by His personal engagement in the details of it. The Lord says in verse 12:

> *A land for which the LORD your God cares; the eyes of the LORD your God are always on it, from the beginning even to the end of the year.*

The Hebrew word for "cares" is *darash*, meaning "… to tread or frequent…."[1] God said His eyes would always be on this land and He was going to walk on it frequently. This was the expectation He set for His people who were going to this new land. Today believers in the marketplace can have this same kind of expectation for God's involvement when we create an atmosphere for the presence of God to dwell.

Through Moses, the Lord said He would attend to watering their crops by providing carefully targeted rainfall known as the early rain and the late rain (Deut. 11:14: *"…He will give the rain for your land in its season, the early and late rain…"*). God said He would cause grass to grow for their herds so that His people would be filled (verse 15: *"He will give grass in your fields for your cattle, and you will eat and be satisfied"*).

## The Expectation of God's Involvement

Moses told the people that they could expect God's involvement in all the elements of this new nation that would be formed in the Promised Land. God would handpick their government leaders and equip them with His anointing to lead His chosen people. He would set up their educational system. He would bless their herds and cause the grass to grow to feed those herds. He would bless their land to produce crops. He would bless their families, their ministry leaders, and their justice system because of His great mercy and love for His people. God would bless their economy and all the elements of their culture.

By God's presence with His people, and this unprecedented level of involvement in all the elements of their culture, His people would be unique from all others. His presence would be their mark of distinction. This mark of distinction was given so that the peoples of the earth would see the power and mercy of the Most High God.

Through the Torah, God established this new culture for His people. This culture included not only the priesthood, but also the farmer, the merchant, the teacher, the judge, fathers and mothers, the general, and the foot soldier. The Lord set one condition for His presence that would produce these tangible benefits of service to the Most High God—obedience to His Word.

The opportunity to enter a new kind of freedom and an unprecedented level of provision in a land God had reserved for His people was largely rejected by most of the generation that died in the wilderness. Many of that generation, though they had been supernaturally liberated from bondage and slavery, still had the mindset of a generation in bondage.

They were experiencing the daily supernatural provision of God through daily manna, and they witnessed the manifest presence of the Living God guiding them through the desert with the pillar of fire and a pillar of cloud. Yet they continued with the mindset of slaves. Because they were still thinking like the slaves of Egypt, they could not take dominion over the land and subdue it. They could not overcome the obstacles to conquest. Those who thought like slaves could not become the formidable army that was necessary to take a land that had already been given to them. Because of this mindset, God raised up a new generation that understood the potential of having the distinction Moses spoke about. Today, we speak with the same God Moses talked with.

## SERVING GOD IN BUSINESS?

A few years ago I was in Ghana, West Africa, holding a MarketPlace Leadership Conference. A young man in his mid-20s came up to me at the break and told me an interesting story. He had become a believer in Jesus while in college, had graduated with a degree in business, and had gone on to Bible college. He said all he wanted to do was serve God. He was certain that he couldn't serve God in the business world, though he had a deep interest in business.

He was within a few months of graduating and began having a gnawing feeling that this wasn't the right thing for him. He said, "I kept telling my friends I didn't think God called me to be a pastor. They all said I was backsliding because you can't serve God in business. After this morning's session, I now understand this is a calling—I have to bring God's Kingdom into the marketplace! Today, God has given me the direction I have been seeking Him for. I can serve Him in business!"

Another generation of people is coming who are beginning to understand this calling to the marketplace. They are asking questions like, "How can His people who serve God in the marketplace be distinguished from those who serve other gods? What can we do to bring in the Kingdom of God?"

The fact that they are even asking those questions is a sign of a change that will come. There is a key to finding the release we are all seeking from the Lord. The answers are the same today as for that nation of farmers—His presence. We must believe that He will do what He says

He will do. We must believe He will bless our fields, our herds, our businesses, our governments, our educational systems, our children, and our marriages—not just our churches. He will do this because He never changes.

It is time for us to understand that the kind of blessing we seek comes from the hand of God, not our own hand.

## THE STOREHOUSE OF WISDOM

You may ask, "How can all these things be?" The answer is simple: we have more resources available to us than all other people have. God has made available to us a storehouse of wisdom and insight. It is not only available to your pastors, but it is available to men and women in business and government as well. I have found that pastors know how to get this wisdom, while many of the people in the marketplace aren't aware God has this wisdom available. I can tell you that God knows everything, and He is willing to share that information with you.

Proverbs 2:7-8 says:

*He stores up sound wisdom for the upright; He is a shield to those who walk in integrity, guarding the paths of justice, and He preserves the way of His godly ones.*

God's storehouse of creative wisdom is there for those who choose to live a life of integrity before God. When we first understand the resources God makes available to us, we then can capitalize on those resources.

The wisdom of God is practical, and it is given to His people to bring about concrete results. As we make a withdrawal from this storehouse, the following things occur: God's wisdom in us will produce tangible results in our work lives; we will make fewer mistakes; our judgment and decision-making capacity will improve because we are collaborating with the Holy Spirit; and we will know things it would otherwise be impossible to know. We walk in greater blessing (as God defines blessing) and we move to positions of leadership because leaders look for emerging leaders with the characteristics of good judgment and insight.

The gifts of the Holy Spirit were never meant to be on display solely in the church house. We have to change our thinking and begin to expect the gifts of the Holy Spirit to operate in a board meeting of a Fortune 500 company, or on a coffee plantation in Central America.

God gave these gifts to us to be utilized in the marketplace. There is a big difference between hoping for these gifts and expecting their full operation for any situation. God has given us the tools to function at the highest level in our workplace. In the days ahead, those who understand this concept will find themselves moving to positions of influence. They will have an anointing for the marketplace. Can it possibly be that an anointing is available to people in the business world or in government? The answer is yes!

## How This Anointing Operates

Let me explain how this kind of anointing operates in the marketplace. Jim is a land developer who has a well-deserved reputation as a creative deal maker. He is gifted when it comes to making dead deals come to life or complicated deals simple. His partners are astute businessmen, yet they are constantly amazed at the sound creativity he displays. One day I asked Jim how he comes up with these creative ideas.

He said, "I can't possibly come up with these things myself. I work hard on them and take them as far as I can. Then, before I go to bed, I pray, 'Lord, I can't take this deal any further. If You don't help us, it doesn't look like it can happen.' Psalm 127:2 tells us, *'It is vain for you to rise up early, to retire late, to eat the bread of painful labors; for He gives to His beloved even in his sleep.'* Would You show me how to do this while I sleep? Invariably the Lord will wake me in the early morning and I go to my computer and I see the whole thing before my eyes, every detail. The Lord shows me these creative, complicated ways to make the deal happen."

My observations of this man and this process over the years is that these deals, however big or small, are never driven by self-interest or selfish ambition but by what honors God and by what is best for every party involved in the deal.

What a unique way of conducting business! Yet this is the only way to conduct business in the Kingdom culture. The Lord collaborates with this kind of approach. His presence and partnership are the marks of distinction that Moses spoke about. As we meet His criteria and seek Him with a whole heart, we open up an entirely new paradigm of God's creativity. Many are operating in this kind of marketplace anointing. For others, it will require some changes.

## ACTIVITY/PRESENCE

One morning the Lord woke me very early to pray. This has been a regular occurrence for me over the years and the part of my day that I cherish. I had been struggling, however, with what I perceived as a decreased activity level in my life. For over 20 years, I had run a demanding business, and at God's direction, I began a process of re-structuring my life to spend more time in prayer, study, writing, and fulfilling the two assignments He gave me in the mid-90s. In many ways, this was my time of activation, so to speak.

It took me over a year to make this transition. I no longer had the same level of business activity or the demands on my time that I had lived with for a long time. I was faced with fewer cell phone calls, emails, decisions, deadlines, daily pressures, and a less-demanding schedule. However, this was a more difficult transition than I had expected. Though I still had a busy schedule because I was spending more time praying and studying, I had the mistaken perception that less business activity of this kind equated to less value, less significance.

That morning the Lord said two words, *activity* and *presence*. I pondered those words for some time and finally asked the Lord if He would explain what they meant. (Over the years I have discovered that it has been much more fruitful for me to ask questions of the Lord rather than make statements to Him.) He said something that has profoundly impacted my life: "Activity will never produce My presence. My presence will always produce focused, productive activity."

## TIME IN HIS PRESENCE

I hear one statement consistently from busy leaders, no matter what nation they are from, no matter what level of responsibility or leadership they have. It is said in many different ways and for many different reasons, but always it is the same phrase: "I don't have time to be alone with God every day." "I'm too busy!" "You don't know my schedule."

I have heard all the reasons, and I have even tried to convince myself with a few of them in years past. But Moses said it best in Exodus 33:15, *"...If Your presence does not go with us, do not lead us up from here."*

It was too dangerous for Moses and the Jews to be left to their own wisdom and insight on their journey, and it is too dangerous for us as well. Time in His presence every day is not an option for us—it is a necessity. You need the wisdom and insight God has for you, and you will find it in the greatest measure when you set aside time to be alone with Him on a daily basis.

God doesn't need time with you; you need time with Him. Not having a time alone with Him on a daily basis won't make Him love you any less. However, it will prevent you from gaining a deeper level of sanctified judgment or decision-making capacity that will enable you to be distinguished from your peers. Besides the character of God in His people, there must be "something" that will distinguish us from everyone else on the face of the earth. That "something" Moses correctly discerned is still the presence of God.

## GOD HAS SECRETS

God has all the knowledge you need to invest, manage, lead, educate, heal, or decide. King David wrote in Psalm 25:14, *"The secret of the LORD is for those who fear Him, and He will make them know His covenant."* God has secrets—all kinds of secrets about all kinds of things! These "secrets" cannot be known by natural means or natural wisdom because God has hidden them. The apostle Paul said in Colossians 2:2-3 (NKJV), *"…to the knowledge of the mystery of God, both of the Father and of Christ, in whom are hidden all the treasures of wisdom and knowledge."*

The good part about all this is that the Lord is willing to reveal those secrets to us. I have discovered that God's secrets have usually been revealed to me in those early morning times when I am alone with Him, where no distraction competes for my time. Worship is a big component of these times because worship creates the atmosphere for God's presence.

This does not mean that God will give His insight and wisdom on a subject only under these conditions. Certainly He will give us wisdom during the day when we ask Him. However, we tap into a much deeper level of His knowledge when we carve out time to just sit in His presence to worship and listen. As you position yourself to have time in His presence, you will find that the by-product of His presence will be "…focused, productive activity," just as He spoke to me.

# HOW DO YOU DO THIS?

The question then becomes, "How do you do this?" Here are some simple suggestions that will bring you some profound results. Some of them aren't original to me. I've listened to many godly men and women in my life who have helped me formulate a lifestyle in which I learned to live before the Lord daily. Find out what works for you, then decide to do it. I offer these suggestions as a guideline:

- Set aside time daily to meet with the Lord. Begin with a structured time, just like a meeting on your calendar. Ask God to meet with you that morning. Ask Him to direct your study of His Word. *"Establish my footsteps in Your word, and do not let any iniquity have dominion over me"* (Ps. 119:133). Ask Him lots of questions and listen for His answers. You may have to go to bed earlier at night to meet with Him. Do whatever it takes!

- Don't get discouraged if your room doesn't fill with the light of Heaven every morning. It is more important to be faithful to the commitment of time. Rest assured you will be changed as you spend time with Him. It is impossible not to be changed. The Lord won't waste His time or yours. I assure you He will honor your commitment to Him.

- Bring work issues before Him and ask the Lord for His insight. It is not unspiritual to ask God to bless your business or your workplace. If you are in business, ask Him to bless the business. Ask Him to show you how to make it better. Ask Him to give you His wisdom so you can be a better manager or employee. If you are in government, ask Him to give you wisdom to govern. Bring these things to Him and then just sit and listen. I have learned to set aside all the "issues" that may be pressing me and just tell the Lord, "If You have anything You want to say to me this morning, Lord, I'll listen." Then I just wait, worship, and study with the ear of my spirit heavenward.

• Keep a journal. I have done this most of my Christian life. It is like a history of my life in God. I keep the notebooks because it gives me the "global perspective" of my life in Christ. I write down things I ask the Lord; I list my concerns with business or family. This has become a treasure to me. Each year I change notebooks.

• Practice seasons of fasting and prayer. Everyone is different when it comes to fasting. For some it is physically not possible to fast. You can meet with the Lord in other ways. For the rest of us, however, do not be too easy on yourself. I have found that fasting, particularly long fasts, enable me to walk in the presence of God in deep ways. The first three days are always challenging for me, but at a certain point food becomes unimportant and the lines of communication with Heaven are wide open. Again, it is OK to fast and pray for your business. The Lord is just as engaged in your business as He is in your church. He wants your fields to grow and your herds to multiply.

• Set aside days of prayer and fasting for your business or your place of employment. If you are responsible to manage people and can't take the time off, do what you can. If you are an employee, work, pray, and fast. The Hebrew word *"avodah"* is a word that means both work and worship. The idea is that on specific days you go before the Lord fasting and praying for your place of employment. If possible, clear the slate of everything and just be in an attitude of prayer during the day. This is something that may work better for business or government leaders, though it is available to all of us in some fashion. Find what works for you, then do it.

# PRACTICAL APPLICATION

Years ago, the Lord told me I was to set aside one afternoon a month to be alone, away from my office, with no cell phone, and to pray only for my business, nothing else. To me this was a revolutionary concept. I had never heard of such a thing. I always thought that God had a passing interest in my business, but His real concern was with "spiritual" things. This is how many of us are programmed to think, but nothing is further from the truth. I almost felt guilty that first day, because it seemed so "unspiritual" to even consider praying for a business—but I obeyed. That obedience not only changed my business but also my life. This is one of God's "secrets." My afternoon grew to one day of fasting and prayer per month. The Lord told me I was to set aside a day during the workweek because it was to be a sacrifice for me.

For some, this arrangement may not be possible, and again, I offer it only as a suggestion. The day I set aside always ended up being the day I had to contend for. Crises abounded. I had to learn to prioritize and deal with the crisis at another time. Many times I used to have the feeling that I was stumbling into that day with a sense of desperation to hear what God had to say about things. At the end of the day I had a sense of peace and direction.

In the morning I would list, on separate pieces of paper, issues or business deals that needed God's wisdom. I would lay my hands on these papers, commit them to the Lord, and ask Him to speak about these things. I would worship, study my Bible, and just wait for the Lord to speak. During the day, the Lord would begin to give me impressions about these issues and I would write them down on these papers.

I have had the Lord speak to me about details in my business I could never have known. Sometimes He would speak about attitudes of my employees that I needed to correct. Often my own attitude was what needed correcting. Sometimes He would speak about deals He was bringing to me.

This day became one that I learned to cherish, but one I needed to fight for. Over the years I learned that God knew everything about my business, and He was willing to reveal some of His knowledge about it as I spent time away from everything but Him.

On one occasion, one of the issues was advertising. I told the Lord the business belonged to Him and I didn't know how to advertise His business. If He wanted to get the name of His business in front of the people in our region, He would have to show me how. Within nine months I was invited four times on television programs that focused on my segment of residential construction to talk about my company. I also wrote magazine articles and international publications about my company or the products of my company. At no time did I ask for this or pay for the advertisement. I grew to love this day! God knows everything, and He can do anything.

# DO GOD AND BUSINESS REALLY MIX?

I hear one thing consistently from younger marketplace believers in many nations: "The fathers (older, successful Christian business and government leaders) are telling us God and business don't mix." I will categorically state that this is a false perception, though a prevalent one. There are only two possible reasons for this statement. These are either the words of one who honestly does not understand or one who lives his life outside of the will of God. Nothing could be further from the truth than to say that God and business don't mix!

God will not "mix" with those who don't walk by His standards of integrity and righteousness in their business dealings. Those who won't walk in His standards of integrity don't want God involved in their businesses. In that regard, this statement is true: God and that kind of business won't mix. His standards, as outlined in His Word, will always produce His presence and therefore His involvement. As Moses said, it is His presence that makes us different from everyone else.

God's desire is still the same today—to distinguish His people from all others because of His presence. Whether you are in government, business, education, medicine, finance, the media, sports, or ministry, He has limitless resources available to you. He knows everything there is to know and more about business (He set up His own economic system); medicine (He created the human body); psychology (He's the Wonderful Counselor); government (the government rests on His shoulders); ministry (He is the Good Shepherd); farming; computers; strategic planning; science; etc. He is willing to serve as our Consultant and give us His expertise, but He won't pursue us; we must pursue Him.

## WE CREATE THE ATMOSPHERE FOR HIS PRESENCE

As we create the atmosphere for His presence by integrity in our business dealings, times of worship, obedience to His known will, and justice in dealing with others, God will be fully engaged with us in the marketplace. If you are in sales and you lie to your customers and manipulate them into purchasing your product for your own self-interest, don't expect this kind of engagement from God in your business. He does not collaborate with manipulation.

George is a man with a "gift" for sales. This is the will of God for his life. He is a man of God who lives a life of prayer and consecration to God's standards of integrity. George and his wife have been tested in ways that would cause most of us to crumble. Yet I have watched in amazement how this testing has strengthened his love for God and people. He is an example of a man who walks in the grace of God. George has won many awards for his excellence and has a national reputation in his field.

George said, "For 23 years, God has always prospered me. It has been amazing because even when my colleagues struggled, God has always caused me to prosper. In my business the Lord has shown me that there are several keys: 1) Hold God accountable to His Word. If I am doing everything I can do, I just remind the Lord what His Word says. 2) Give tithes and offerings and practice generosity toward others. Generosity includes my time and money. 3) Never compromise integrity for money. I chase God not money. 4) Wait on Him. You can't rush Him to make something happen; you can only wait. 5) Don't try to hide manipulation. The people who are worth manipulating understand manipulation. Anything gained through manipulation has a very short-term gain."

George is an example of how men and women around the world can succeed, as God defines success, by walking in the principles of the Word for the marketplace. His principles and His presence are not just for Sunday. God intended for His people to live in His presence Monday through Saturday as well. God's presence produces tangible benefits. This is the by-product of the distinguishing mark Moses spoke about.

In the coming days, the Lord will be giving great resources into the hands of marketplace people around the world. These resources will be given for the purpose of funding Kingdom strategies. These strategies may mean funding ministries or churches, but they also may mean funding farming cooperatives so godly farmers in developing countries can get a fair price for their products. They may mean funding vast crusades and missionaries, but they may also mean buying medicines and food for the poor. These are resources that come with responsibility.

Marketplace people must begin to understand the secrets of the Kingdom Economy in order to understand the resource of God's wisdom and insight that is available to His people. Then we will be able to administer God's resources with the level of integrity that He requires.

ENDNOTE

1.  James Strong, STD, LLD, *A Concise Dictionary of the Words in the Hebrew Bible* (Madison, NJ: Strong, 1890), 31.

# CHAPTER 2

## *Questions for Consideration*

1. Have you ever wondered what the distinction is between you and others in your workplace who may not know God?

_____

_____

_____

_____

_____

2. Do you believe God desires His presence to dwell in your workplace? What would be the result in your life if He did?

_____

_____

_____

_____

_____

_____

_____

_____

3. In your mind, do God and business mix? Are you comfortable with His involvement and direction in your business?

_____

_____

_____

_____

_____

4. When was the last time you experienced God's wisdom in your life? Did you acknowledge that God was the source of this wisdom?

_____

_____

_____

_____

_____

_____

_____

5. Have you ever asked God to give you a creative business idea?

_____

_____

_____

_____

_____

_____

_____

_____

# CHAPTER 3

## Equal Responsibility, Equal Anointing—The Two Pillars

*Thus he set up the pillars at the porch of the nave; and he set up the right pillar and named it Jachin, and he set up the left pillar and named it Boaz* (1 Kings 7:21).

Many pastors are sincerely searching for a better understanding of the critical relationship between the marketplace and professional ministry. Pastors are not alone in this search. Believers all over the world, whether they sit in the pews or occupy the pulpits, at some time in their lives struggle with understanding just how God wants us all to fit together for the purposes of His Kingdom. People in the pews may have a call to ministry, but it may not be to professional, pulpit ministry.

This kind of call can bring about a confusing time, particularly for believers in business, government, education, etc. (the marketplace). Many who feel this desire for a deeper life of effectiveness for the Lord are sincerely trying to hear the Lord. They often wonder if they should quit their jobs and become pastors or join the staff of their churches.

The answer is that we are to be led by the Spirit of God. Each of us needs to find the role that God has for us. We should not be led by discomfort with our present circumstances or by our desire to minister but by our commitment to the plan of God for our lives. We have to understand our specific roles and stay in those roles until He brings promotion. Personal discomfort has very little to do with being led by the Spirit of God. If a person's role is that of a pastor, then he or she must walk in that role. But if that role is an entrepreneur, then he or she must walk in that role with the same honor and zeal.

## THE MYTHICAL LADDER

We sometimes think in terms of a mythical ladder we must climb to "really please God." The bottom rung of the ladder is the marketplace (business, government, etc.), which is often referred to as "secular work" or "working for money." To reach the top rung of this ladder, which represents service to God, we must leave the marketplace and become pastors or missionaries.

When we think like this, we live with two misconceptions. The first misconception is that we think God's involvement in our work life is minimal; therefore our accountability to Him is also minimal. If God is not really that involved with us, then it doesn't really matter if we lack integrity from time to time. If He only becomes fully engaged with the "sacred" and we are at the bottom ("secular") rung of this mythical ladder, we are more or less left to our own devices with marginal involvement from God.

The Scripture dispels this misconception. *"Whatever you do, do your work heartily, as for the Lord rather than for men"* (Col. 3:23). Everything we do during the workday is holy to the Lord. It does not matter whether we pastor a church or clean a toilet; whether we are a missionary, an ambassador, or a ditch digger. According to Colossians 3, it is all holy to Him. He cares about it all, from how hard we work to our punctuality and integrity and the respect of those in authority over us. We represent Him to the world Monday through Saturday. He is fully engaged all the time in everything we do, whether it is the worship service at church or leading a stockholders' meeting at a Fortune 500 company. He is looking for an exhibition of our character (His character in us) in all these things.

The second misconception is that we must move from "secular work" to the "sacred work" in order to get to the top of this mythical ladder. I remember after the first segment at one of our MarketPlace Leadership Conferences in El Salvador, a pastor in his 50s came up to me and he was crying. He told me about his deep desire to serve God and minister to people. He said he had been a businessman for many years but had a business failure a number of years ago. He thought that this failure meant that he was probably doing the wrong thing and God wanted him to be a pastor. He thought it would not be possible to serve God as a businessman, so he went into the professional ministry.

He was embraced by some ministry colleagues as one who had finally "seen the light," and eventually he became a pastor of a church. Even though he was a pastor, he continued this love and deep interest of business. He confessed to me that he had struggled to find fulfillment and effectiveness in this role as pastor. He said the Lord had spoken to him during that first segment of our conference that he was never "called" to this role of a pastor, but God had indeed "called" him to business. He told me that he now understood that he was meant to serve God with the same zeal and passion in business. He raised his hands to Heaven, wept for joy, and said, "Gloria a Dios!"

## GOD KNOWS HOW MANY PASTORS THE WORLD NEEDS

The world needs pastors, and marketplace people need pastors. The Kingdom will not function without them. They care for our souls and, by God's design, they have a special place in every culture. But God knows how many pastors the world needs, so He equips just the right number for every generation. If you are not equipped emotionally and spiritually to be a pastor, you will have a very difficult job trying to fulfill that role over the long term. The broader viewpoint is that God's people, who need the care of one of His pastors, will not get what they need. You will eventually flourish when you find the role you have been divinely equipped to fulfill, whether that is as a pastor, a homemaker, or an entrepreneur.

Many people in the marketplace who have a heart to serve God find themselves confused about these issues. We don't seem to be getting the message to the Body of believers worldwide that it is perfectly appropriate and necessary for men and women to serve God in the marketplace if this is God's role for them.

The issue for all of us to ask ourselves is, "What is my role?" When God calls us to a role, whatever that role is, we have been divinely equipped by Him for that specific role. Only in that role will we become most effective and find lasting fulfillment.

Failure in that role does not necessarily mean God is moving you to "full-time ministry" or the "sacred." It may mean you are doing some things wrong and corrections need to be made. It may also mean you are in a time of testing. Isaiah recorded God's viewpoint on such matters in Isaiah 55:8-9:

> *"For My thoughts are not your thoughts, nor are your ways My ways," declares the LORD. "For as the heavens are higher than the earth, so are My ways higher than your ways and My thoughts than your thoughts."*

These are well-known verses, but they apply to all areas of life, including the marketplace. God defines success and failure in different terms than we do. What we consider failure, many times He may consider as a character development process. It is our character that God places the highest value on, not success— as we define success. He has a different standard of measurement.

# FILLED WITH WISDOM, KNOWLEDGE, AND SPIRIT

Exodus 35:31 (NKJV) says, *"And He has filled him with the Spirit of God, in wisdom and understanding, in knowledge and all manner of workmanship."* In this verse Moses is speaking about two men who have been supernaturally filled by God to lead the construction of the Tabernacle. They were divinely equipped with skill, knowledge, and understanding. While these men were given the abilities to perform the highly skilled work of artisans for the Tabernacle, they were also supernaturally given management and administrative gifts. They were given intelligence, understanding, and insight (see Exod. 31:1-6). The Lord told Moses in these verses about Bezalel, *"See, I have called by name Bezalel....I have filled him with the Spirit of God, in wisdom, in understanding, in knowledge...."*

This is not unique to this man. Everything we do is "sacred" and God is fully engaged in all work that is performed. Therefore we are accountable to Him for our dealings in business, the decisions we make in government, and the procedures we perform as surgeons, as well as the messages we preach as pastors.

## MOVE TOWARD—NOT AWAY FROM

It is sometimes difficult for marketplace people to realize that God loves us no matter what our performance level is, and nothing will ever change that. This dear brother in El Salvador moved away from his business failure as a defeated man and toward the next stage of his life, hoping God would be pleased with him as a pastor.

When he struggled in that role also, he felt he was of little value to the Lord. This is a common misunderstanding.

Years ago the Lord spoke to me one morning during my prayer time about moving through the different stages of my life. We all have stages or seasons in life as we grow in spiritual maturity and responsibility. We may change jobs, change cities, or have new responsibilities, but change is a part of our life in Christ. Our character determines how well we handle this change. God gave me a bit of His wisdom at a time I needed it. Regarding the changing seasons of my life, He said, "Move **toward** a new season, rather than **away from** one." It is better to move *toward* the next season of life rather than *away from* the previous one.

This may sound like a play on words, but I found it to be a very valuable lesson of life. When the Lord brought about the transitions in my life, I saw that it was important for me to leave one season of my life in victory, having completed my assignment, and be ready for the challenges of the next season. Of course, we are to make these moves by the leading of the Holy Spirit and never because they look like a better deal. Romans 8:14 says, *"For all who are being led by the Spirit of God, these are sons of God."*

This verse has practical application to these specific stages or seasons of life we are talking about. We don't move through these stages having failed, hoping for something better in the next one. I want to stress here that even if others look at your situation as an absolute failure and defeat, you know whether you have conquered and are ready to move on. You can't measure your progress in this journey of life by other people—only by your obedience to the Holy Spirit. You may feel bruised from the fight, but Ephesians 6:13 (NKJV) says, *"Therefore take up the whole armor of God, that you may be able to withstand in the evil day, and having done all, to stand."*

If anyone knew about being bruised and standing, the apostle Paul did. He was whipped, beaten, imprisoned multiple times, and shipwrecked, yet he continued fulfilling his assignment. I wonder if Paul's friends ever said, "You need to find a new job! This one is going to kill you!" Paul was more qualified than most men to say *"…and having done everything, to stand firm"* (Eph. 6:13). Sometimes the victory I am speaking about is found in just standing.

However, when that change comes, whether you are choosing it or someone is choosing it for you, stand and find something to claim a victory over. Don't permit yourself to change a season feeling defeated, and don't worry about what others may think. We have to please only One!

## THE UNDERSTANDING GAP

What is God's model? Many marketplace people are not quite sure where they fit in this Kingdom of God. We thrive in the world of government or business, yet we have a desire to please the Lord with our lives. How could God care about any occupation other than "real" ministry? How do we find our place? How do we bridge this "understanding gap" to be released to do what we are called to do, whatever that calling may be?

God is giving understanding to some church and marketplace leaders. At the same time, He is activating people in their congregations with strategies to bring Jesus Christ to the world in unique ways. Marketplace people are being positioned to transform and lead businesses and governments. They realize that financial resources usually come with strategies to bring the Kingdom to cities, regions, and nations.

## Solomon's Temple

King Solomon was building the first Temple of the Lord. The details of this Temple were drawn up by Solomon's father, King David, with the prophet Nathan. David had it in his heart to build this Temple for the Lord, but he was judged to have shed too much blood, so the task was given to his son Solomon. The Porch of the Nave was a covered entrance to this magnificent structure. Two massive, identical bronze columns were set at the entrance of the porch. Scholars say they were set before the entrance as *"pillars of witness,"* or *"pillars of remembrance."*

Since the prophet Nathan was involved in the plans for the Temple, it is reasonable to assume that God had His hand in the details. Each carving, every detail of the Temple, had significance to the priests and Levites and to the people. Why were these two identical bronze pillars set at the entrance of the Temple so that every worshiper would be called to "remembrance?" Why would the Lord want these pillars so prominently displayed? What did God want us to remember? What were they a "witness" to? Who were the two men these massive columns were named for? Why did they have their names on these columns?

## Who Were These Men?

The first pillar was named Jachin which means "He shall establish"[1] He was an honored priest during the reign of King David. It is significant that Jachin was a priest. However, we will focus on the second pillar named *Boaz* which means "In it is strength."[2] Boaz was a wealthy landowner from Bethlehem. I had understood Boaz to be a successful farmer and a respected businessman, but I was determined to know more about this man who would have a pillar named after him in the most important structure in Jewish history.

I must confess to some skepticism as I explored these verses. I thought about the "Bricks of Faith" concept—that it may have been practiced even in Solomon's day. This practice says things like, "Buy 100 'Bricks of Faith' for the building of our new church (or other endeavor) and your name will be placed in a small plaque. Buy 10,000 Bricks of Faith and we will give you a bronze column with your name on it!" As I read these verses, I pictured Solomon going to this wealthy businessman and saying, "Boaz, if you 'donate' a large amount of shekels to the Temple, we will have your name inscribed on the pillar at the entrance of the Temple. Then everyone will remember you and the offerings you gave."

Sometimes people in the marketplace love to have their names engraved on things. The more "bricks of faith" we buy, the bigger our names get carved on stones for all to see. I tell you, this is the antithesis of everything

I know about Kingdom leadership. As I read these verses, I thought to myself, "Boaz must have paid a great deal for this massive bronze pillar to carry his name."

## Boaz, a Man of Integrity

However, my initial thoughts about Boaz were completely wrong. Boaz was not a contemporary of Solomon but had lived almost 250 years earlier. He was Solomon's great, great grandfather. So respected was this successful farmer/businessman that we are still talking about him thousands of years later. He was a godly man of such integrity, honor, and high moral character that the Lord chose him to be an ancestor of the Messiah. Boaz was a true representative of a biblical culture for business who expressed kindness to the alien and afforded privileges to Ruth the Moabite even though she was not a Jew.

> *The Levite, because he has no portion or inheritance among you, and the alien, the orphan and the widow who are in your town, shall come and eat and be satisfied, in order that the LORD your God may bless you in all the work of your hand which you do* (Deuteronomy 14:29).

Boaz became Ruth's "kinsman redeemer," a term used to describe the work of Jesus on the cross.

## A Blessing Declared

In Ruth 2:4, we see Boaz as a prominent landowner and leader in the city, pronouncing a blessing as a greeting over field hands. In most businesses from the beginning of time until today, this kind of worker goes unnoticed by management and certainly by business owners.

> *Now behold, Boaz came from Bethlehem and said to the reapers, "May the Lord be with you." And they said to him, "May the Lord bless you."*

Not only was he greeting his lowest level workers, but he declared the prayerful blessing of the Lord over them! This was a grateful, godly man who paid attention to the small things. He displayed such high moral integrity and generosity that he remains an example to us today.

## Righteousness Out of the View of Others

On the night Ruth asked Boaz to be her kinsman redeemer, this important yet humble man made a righteous, moral decision because of his fear of the Lord. He had to choose immorality or righteousness and obedience to God's law. If he had chosen the former, he would have become faceless and nameless in history. Because he chose righteousness when no one was present but Ruth the Moabite, an alien, he is revered not only in Jewish history but even today! The study of the Book of Ruth is also a study of Boaz.

How many of us make small, seemingly private decisions on a daily basis that grieve the Lord and disqualify us from our place in history? He wants the whole person to serve Him, not just the man or woman who sits in church on Sunday. He wants us to represent Him in business, socially, in our families, and with our spouses and children.

We are expected to be the Lord's representative in every area of our lives, every day.

## Trade Routes of the Kingdom Economy Must Be Pure!

These two pillars of equal size, weight, and prominence, the "pillars of remembrance," communicated to the worshipers in the Temple equal responsibility before the Lord to implement His purposes. They were a reminder that the character of a person, whether he or she is a priest or a businessperson, is what has lasting significance to the Lord.

These two pillars remind us that leadership, in God's eyes, is not a function of whether one is a priest or in business. The kind of leadership that brings transformation to a culture must come from the core of a man or woman who has been transformed. You can't institute real change if you haven't been changed yourself. Character and commitment to our purpose are the things that qualify us for a life of significance.

These two identical pillars were named for different individuals who had different roles in Jewish history, yet equal responsibility to the Lord for their personal integrity and character. Both represented a model for moral excellence and righteousness that is necessary for any leader God can use.

Today, leaders like Boaz are skilled people who are forming holy alliances that will generate funding for the Kingdom. This is nothing new to the Lord. He has given us models in Scripture that we are rediscovering. The "two pillars" are such a model.

## E N D N O T E S

1.  *The Wycliffe Bible Commentary* (Chicago: Moody Bible Institute, 1962), 318

2.  Ibid.

# CHAPTER 3

## *Questions for Consideration*

1. Do you ever feel like you have to climb that "mythical ladder" to be pleasing to God?

_____

_____

_____

_____

_____

_____

2. Where is your passion? Your passion just may reveal your "calling."

_____

_____

_____

_____

_____

_____

_____

_____

_____

3. Have you ever left one season of your life feeling like a failure and gone into another season hoping for something better?

_____

_____

_____

_____

_____

_____

4. Can you honestly say, "I know God's love for me is not based on my performance level or occupation?"

_____

_____

_____

_____

_____

_____

_____

5. Have you ever considered that serving God with integrity and passion in your professional life is just as pleasing to Him as preaching on Sunday morning?

_____

_____

_____

_____

_____

_____

# CHAPTER 4

## Leaders Must Go Outside the Camp

*Now Moses used to take the tent and pitch it outside the camp, a good distance from the camp, and he called it the tent of meeting. And everyone who sought the LORD would go out to the tent of meeting which was outside the camp.... Thus the LORD used to speak to Moses face to face, just as a man speaks to his friend. When Moses returned to the camp, his servant Joshua, the son of Nun, a young man, would not depart from the tent* (Exodus 33:7,11).

If I told you that the wisdom to solve the difficult challenges that you face was available to you in a particular place every morning, would you come to that place? If I told you that there was a place where you could obtain secrets about your business, family, or organization that would bring success, would you go there to find them? If I said there was a place where you could go to find peace in the midst of your turmoil, wisdom for raising your children, acceptance in the midst of all your rejection, practical insight into your finances, and creative solutions for every one of life's problems, would you run to that place?

Would that place have value to you? The answer to all these questions and many more is obvious. That place is available to all of us, and I can tell you from personal experience, you will find all of the above and much more in that place. You will find that place "outside the camp." It is a place of solitude where you can meet God. It is a place of worship and study. It is a place where the One True God can reach down from Heaven and pour His life and insight into you. It is a wonderful place, and it is the place that all leaders must find every day.

## INSPIRED LEADERSHIP

When crisis comes to a nation, God will raise up a leader to be His voice. When a crisis occurs in a business or a government, God will raise up a leader. When transition from the existing paradigm to a new level of freedom for God's people is about to take place, God will once again raise up a leader.

The leaders who help with this transition aren't always the ones with the loudest voices or the most influence. They usually are not the most obvious. Most of the time they are reluctant but obedient bondservants. They may be overlooked by others. We see this when Samuel prayed his way through Jessie's sons looking for the next king of Israel, who happened to be David, the youngest (see 1 Sam. 16). However, God's leaders have always had an aroma about their lives that comes from time in His presence. This aroma is a by-product of worship, prayer, and the presence of God.

While some of God's leaders may not be so obvious to us in the beginning, there are others who are born to lead. We can watch children at play to observe this dynamic. One of the children sets the rules of the game for everyone else. This, too, is a gift from God, whether we recognize it as such or not. He determines this kind of characteristic in the heart of people. *"For You created my inmost being; you knit me together in my mother's womb"* (Ps. 139:13 NIV).

The ability to lead people is something that is inborn. Certainly there are techniques and refinements that we can learn to help us be more effective, but the ability to lead people is clearly a gift from God. Many people have been given a gift to lead others on some level, but because of circumstances, negative input from others, timidity, or other factors, their gifts are hindered from developing and they may never exercise the gifts they have been given.

In the Kingdom there is another kind of leader who has the same kind of gift but who also carries the inspiration of the Holy Spirit. These are leaders who are anointed, inspired worshipers who are destined to implement the strategies of the Lord in their day. It is not enough to have a destiny for this kind of thing. We must also accept the cost of that destiny—and there will be a cost.

A leader who is divinely inspired will learn to find the time for inspiration in the presence of the Lord. Divinely inspired leadership, whether in business, government, or ministry, is always filtered through the insight and expertise of the Father.

I have spoken with many people in the marketplace around the world who seem to have great difficulty with the most important aspect of leadership in the Kingdom: time with God. The reasons for not setting aside time with the Lord are always the same, no matter where I go in the world:

"There is just not enough time in my day."

"I don't get anything out of it."

"I'm too busy."

It is always a perception of value that causes this response. We make time in our busy lives for the things that have the highest value. This is always the case.

Time alone with God is basic to life as a believer. Yet, if you are a leader with a destiny to implement God's strategies, time with Him is not optional. Anointed and inspired leaders have to position themselves for the anointing and inspiration. Those things don't come from being self-assured; they come from the Lord. Commitment to this kind of time away from everything will always be contested ground. However, if you are to be a leader in the Kingdom, it is essential that you conquer that ground. You will lead on a lower level if you try to lead without God's insight.

# MOSES HAD NO RESUMÉ

Moses was a man who was appointed by the Lord to leadership at a critical time in the history of God's people. Outwardly, he had few qualifications for the job. He was a fugitive and a shepherd for his father-in-law. He didn't even own the business! When he was appointed to this task by the Lord, the only leadership on his resumé for the previous 40 years was leading sheep.

Moses had been so broken during those 40 years that when the Lord came to him in the burning bush, he said, "You must have the wrong guy. I can't speak to people." Yet when he accepted the task that the Lord set before him, he came to understand something that has been illustrated for us throughout Scripture—all of God's leaders learned to spend time alone with Him to draw from His wisdom to lead others.

Moses knew the only way he could accomplish this task was to draw from God's resource of wisdom and insight. He had been so broken and humbled during his 40 years in the seemingly insignificant role as a shepherd that to the natural eye he was unimportant and insignificant. Shepherds didn't occupy a position of prominence in the culture of the day. He could not go to the Scripture for encouragement, because there was no Scripture. He was alone. What disqualified him for leadership in the eyes of everyone else was the very thing that qualified him in God's eyes. His humility, meekness, and dependence on the Lord afforded him one of the most envied positions in the history of our world—a friend of God.

# Joshua Generation

Not only did Moses communicate regularly with God, *"…just as a man speaks to his friend…"* (Exod. 33:11), but another very important dynamic was taking place. Because the Lord is the ultimate strategic thinker, He is always multigenerational. He allowed Moses to train and mentor the next generation of leaders. Whether Moses knew it or not, God was seeding the next leader of Israel. That leader was Joshua.

In Exodus 33:11, the Hebrew word for "a young man" means Joshua was likely in his teenage years.[1] I have often pictured this scene in Exodus in the following way: Moses would finish conversing with God and Joshua would say, "Moses, the tent of meeting needs cleaning up a bit, so I'll just stay to clean up." The cloud of glory that settled over the entrance of the tent would lift as Moses walked back to the camp, and Joshua would fall on his face in worship, not wanting to leave this place where the tangible presence of God had been. To remain in that place was enough for Joshua.

God must have been pleased that this young man loved His presence so much that he was happy to be where God had been! He was a young man who had the makings of a leader God could trust. Joshua loved the presence of God!

Moses was alone on top of a mountain overlooking the Promised Land when God told him he was going to die. Moses' first response was to ask the Lord on behalf of the people for a leader to succeed him. The Lord already had selected His man to lead Israel. Joshua was now an older man who could be trusted with the leadership of God's most cherished possession, His people. God knew he could be trusted because over the years he had exhibited a desire for the presence of God.

Numbers 27:18 says, *"So the Lord said to Moses, 'Take Joshua the son of Nun, a man in whom is the Spirit, and lay your hand on him.'"* It would be impossible for Joshua to not be designated by God as a "man of the spirit" when he *"...would not depart from the tent"* (Exod. 33:11). God notices this kind of thing in our lives! Times and seasons of history have changed, but God's qualifications for leadership have been a constant. If you are going to be the kind of leader that is anointed and inspired to do great things for Him, you have to carry this designation.

## THE SECRET

So how does this apply to people like us today? The secret of Moses' success was what happened in the tent of meeting. Kingdom leadership, whether it is in government, business, education, or ministry, requires that we spend time with the King. The Kingdom Economy is an economic system that operates by the rules of Heaven. It is a supernatural economy that will have tangible benefits in our lives.

By spending time "outside the camp" we will be distinguished from all other people on the earth. Therefore, it is natural that the enemy of our souls will contend with us for this time. He will try to oppose everything that God wants to do, whether it is establishing a church, sending a missionary, starting a Kingdom business, or educating children. He will try to tear at covenant relationships, and he will come to distract you from your quiet time.

Men and women who think they are "called" to a position of leadership in any capacity must find time to go "outside the camp." It does not matter how busy you are; go outside the camp and draw from the same well of resource that Moses and so many others have found essential.

If you are a leader in government, ministry, or business, it is important to realize that a well of expertise is available for you to draw living water from on a daily basis. This well is filled with practical insight, protection, supernatural understanding of complex issues, and a path to victory that may look like certain defeat to you. You have a "Consultant" available to you who understands everything about everything. Knowing that the commitment to go outside the camp has the potential to transform your business, government, family, or marriage, the real question becomes: Why would you not spend time outside the camp?

## TANGIBLE EFFECTS

Marketplace leaders are usually busy people with high levels of expertise in their given areas. Their time is at a premium. As you take time to go outside the camp, you will see clear, tangible effects on all aspects of your life, including the workplace. You will make fewer mistakes. You will exhibit better judgment. You will have greater insight into future events. You will hear God's voice better and more frequently. When a crisis comes—and crises come to all of us—you will have a greater confidence to make decisions when you spend time outside the camp. The reason is that the Lord wants to provide you with the resources at His disposal. His resources are not just theoretical, but practical and tangible.

Proverbs 16:3 says, *"Commit your works to the Lord and your plans will be established."* The Hebrew word for *works* means "a transaction, a product, a thing made, business, occupation, workmanship."[2] These are the things we do on a daily basis to make a living. The houses we build, the products we sell, the decisions we make as government leaders, the things we produce with our hands or minds.

The Hebrew word here for *plans* means "cunning (work), curious work, imagination, means, purpose, thought."[3] Thoughts and imaginations referred to in this verse are creative and they come from God. When we commit our business, occupation, and workmanship to Him, God's creativity becomes available to us.

## God Is a Shield to His People

My business was the design and construction of homes in a resort area. We had just completed a large home for an executive, and he and his wife were scheduled to move into their new home in a few days. They had expressed their deep appreciation to my staff and me for our work and they asked me to put them on our referral list. They were to close their legal transaction with the mortgage bank on a particular Wednesday at 3:00 p.m.

According to our state laws, if I did not make a legal demand for any funds that were due prior to that closing, I had no immediate legal recourse to the funds. Though my client still owed me $10,000, I had absolutely no concerns about getting the money after having successfully worked with this couple for over one year.

On that same Wednesday morning at 6:00 A.M., I was outside the camp with the Lord reading my Bible, when I heard the Lord say, "He is going to try to cheat you out of that ten thousand dollars." I was so surprised at these words that I said, "Lord, is that You? How can this be? He would never do that." However, I immediately went to my office that morning and phoned my client about the outstanding balance. He laughed and said, "I might pay you Friday or maybe Monday." I realized immediately that the Lord was protecting us.

I phoned his mortgage bank to tell them I was still due $10,000 and I was planning to make that demand and block his closing that afternoon. The banker said, "Call this number immediately" and gave me a number, but he would give me no further information. Without knowing who I was calling, I engaged the gentleman on the other line at 7:15 that morning by introducing myself and briefly explaining that the banker suggested I call him.

The man's response left me speechless. "Mr. Cuny, I do not get involved in situations like this. However, you have built homes for many of our executives and your reputation precedes you. I consider it an honor to speak with you, sir, and I will personally attend to this matter immediately." This man happened to be a senior officer in the company my client worked for. Much to my client's dismay, by 3:00 P.M. that afternoon I had the funds.

My question to you is this: what if I had decided to sleep in that Wednesday morning? How many business deals, wrong decisions, and errors in judgments do we all make because we do not position ourselves outside the camp to listen to the Lord? Going outside the camp is not our religious duty but the opportunity for us to have God's input in our lives. His input will always produce tangible benefits in our lives. For us to function successfully in the Kingdom, the King must be our priority every day.

## GOD MAKES AVAILABLE HIS CREATIVITY

We need to understand that God is creative. He can make something out of nothing—that's creativity. His creativity is not limited to artistic expression, but it extends to business, education, finance, technology, medicine, and government as well. His creativity has no limits or boundaries. We could say He created creativity. The apostle Paul said it much better than I will ever say in Romans 11:33:

*Oh, the depth of the riches both of the wisdom and knowledge of God! How unsearchable are His judgments and unfathomable His ways!*

Paul spoke about something he had experienced personally. When you understand what is waiting for you outside the camp, you will want to live there!

I know several businesspeople who have a reputation of being creative deal makers. Like Jim, whom I mentioned in Chapter 2, these people love to spend time in the presence of the Lord. They spend time in worship, prayer, and study of God's Word. In each case, they attribute this reputation to time with the Lord. They don't presume this creativity comes from natural means. God's desire is to lead us by His Spirit. The question always is, "How do we find the leading of the Spirit?"

Set aside time on a daily basis, away from cell phones, appointments, and the pressures of life, and make yourself available to the Lord. Study His Word, seek His face, and worship Him. Ask Him questions and wait for answers. Commit your works to Him. As you do this, you will find a peace and serene confidence coming over your soul. You will fear the future less and trust God more.

## The How-To's

You may say, "I have struggled with having a quiet time for years." Therein lies the problem: you are struggling. Don't struggle anymore; just surrender. As you spend time with the Lord alone on a daily basis, you will love people more. You will love your spouse more, find greater insight into problems, and have better judgment. You may say, "How can this be?" You will become more like the One you behold. The vision you have for your life will take on the characteristics of the vision that God has for your life. Meeting with God every day will sustain you during the difficult times. He will meet you day by day, sometimes in a quiet way that is barely perceivable. Sometimes His presence will be so real you will not want to leave. Sometimes the Word of God will explode off the page like an atomic bomb. It will transform your life!

When I first began establishing this discipline in my life, I had difficulty with consistency. I zealously told the Lord I would meet Him every morning, and I meant every word of my commitment. One morning I struggled getting up and decided that morning I needed the sleep. When I got up and began getting ready for my day, the Lord gently said to me, "I missed you this morning, son." I was stunned at His words. Those few words changed my life forever because I realized that when I told the Lord I would meet Him, He would also meet with me.

Will He love you less if you don't? Emphatically not! I have discovered that the Lord will always come where His presence is cherished. If you view this time as a religious obligation or duty, you might as well stay in bed. Realize that time with the Lord on a daily basis makes available to you the wisdom of God. That wisdom will distinguish you from others, and you will begin to wake up with expectancy about your meeting. It will become your lifeblood. Moses said the thing that distinguished God's people from all other people was His presence (see Exod. 33:16). When you meet with Him, He will meet with you.

You may say, "I don't have the time." Prioritize your life. You prioritize your life anyway; only now make time with God your number one priority. There is precedent for this. Matthew 6:33 (NKJV) says, *"But seek first the kingdom of God and His righteousness, and all these things shall be added to you."* We all make time for what is important to us. Where you spend your time is where you prioritize your life. The practical aspects of the Kingdom Economy are available for us on a daily basis, but we must walk outside the camp. Remember, it is not a duty we must keep; it is a privilege that has been afforded to us.

You may say, "I can't get up that early." Go to bed earlier. I have a close friend who is an African pastor/leader. He prays six hours a day, every day, starting early in the morning. This man walks in the extraordinary for a reason. He is awake every morning around 2:00 or 3:00 A.M. to sit before the Lord and pray. We can sleep a little less and pray a lot more, and the benefit will be an extraordinary lifestyle. People I know who do great things for the Kingdom understand this principle of time alone with God. They understand that a tangible by-product comes from time with the Lord. If you desire more in your life in God, go outside the camp and get more. Do whatever it takes, but make that walk outside the camp. Your business depends on it, your family depends on it, and your future depends on it!

You may say, "I don't get anything out of it." You get more than you think! When you tell the Lord you want to meet with Him each day, do you think He will be too busy with the administration of Heaven to meet you? He is willing to give you what you need and more. The psalmist wrote, *"The LORD is near to all who call upon Him, to all who call upon Him in truth"* (Ps. 145:18).

## WHY IS THIS IMPORTANT?

Simply put, this is how His Kingdom operates, and we must exercise the will of God in the world we live in—that includes business, government, education, media, the arts, entertainment, and medicine, as well as church. In order to exercise His will, we must know it. In order to know it, we must position ourselves to hear what the Spirit is saying to us.

Jesus said in John 5:19:

*...Truly, truly, I say to you, the Son can do nothing of Himself, unless it is something He sees the Father doing; for whatever the Father does, these things the Son also does in like manner.*

This statement cannot be less true for us than it is for Jesus.

The world wants to follow inspired, anointed leaders who fear God and walk in integrity. This kind of inspiration and anointing comes from time alone with God. Every resource we need is found in Him. All the expertise necessary for us to be a distinguished people in this world is found in Him. You will find the subtle decisions of life that will bring success "outside the camp."

## E N D N O T E S

1. James Strong, S.T.D., LL.D., *A Concise Dictionary of the Words in the Hebrew Bible* (Madison, NJ: Strong, 1890) 70.

2. James Strong, S.T.D., LL.D., *A Concise Dictionary of the Words in the Hebrew Bible,* (Madison, NJ: Strong, 1890), 65.

3. Ibid.

# CHAPTER 4

## *Questions for Consideration*

1. Is there a time in your day when you shut out all the distractions to be alone with God? Explain why or why not.

_____

_____

_____

_____

_____

_____

_____

_____

_____

2. Has God ever given you an "assignment" for which you did not have the appropriate qualifications? Did you lean on Him to help you fulfill the assignment?

_____

_____

_____

_____

_____

_____

_____

3. Have you ever considered that your success as a leader is less about your abilities and more about prioritizing your life so you can receive input from the Lord on how He wants you to lead?

_____

_____

_____

_____

_____

_____

_____

4. If I told you that time "outside the camp" would bring about tangible results in your life, your family, and your work, would you go there?

_____

_____

_____

_____

_____

_____

_____

_____

# CHAPTER 5

## *We Own Nothing—He Owns Everything!*

*For every beast of the forest is Mine, the cattle on a thousand hills. I know every bird of the mountains, and everything that moves in the field is Mine. If I were hungry I would not tell you, for the world is Mine, and all it contains* (Psalm 50:10-12).

God does not have a sense of indebtedness to us. In Psalm 50, His viewpoint on the issue of ownership is stated rather clearly—God owns everything. Yet many of us seem to spend our lifetimes striving for things to "own," and once we get them, we are determined to protect what we have and accumulate more. This kind of striving always brings with it concern about how to keep what we have, or how to protect it from others who may want it. Psalm 50 gives us one of the definitive statements of real ownership in Scripture. This statement reveals the Kingdom perspective.

Haggai 2:8 is another verse that gives even more insight, *"'The silver is Mine and the gold is Mine,' declares the LORD of hosts."* The Scripture is filled with verses such as these. Ownership is a settled matter in the eyes of Heaven, and it needs to be a settled issue with people who want to live in the Kingdom Economy as well. God's ownership is not an ideal to be hoped for; it is a universal reality.

The Lord will not be indebted to us over something He already owns. I have discovered that the Lord will not wrestle with us for control of anything. If we deny this Kingdom reality and choose to retain ownership of anything, He will not challenge us. However, the issue of personal ownership to the believer quickly becomes a burden too heavy to carry. What a different perspective! Yet for marketplace people who choose to live in the Economy of the Kingdom, this is the only valid perspective. Remember, these are principles by which the Kingdom Economy functions. To live under the sovereignty of God is to live in His Kingdom. To live in His Kingdom means conducting ourselves in the marketplace by the principles of the Kingdom Economy. This includes our understanding of ownership.

I have a close friend who has an unusual understanding of this reality. When he came to the revelation that God owned everything, he and his wife wanted to make a declaration to Heaven that all their possessions really belonged to God. They took the deed to their home and walked through each room of their house praying. They said, "Lord, the deed to this house has our names on it, but in reality it is Your house. Thank You for letting us live here in Your house. Lord, the furniture of Your house, we acknowledge today it belongs to You also. The clothes are Yours as well. Lord, we want You to know everything we have is Yours. We agree with You that all this belongs to You."

This may sound like a radical approach, but it is merely agreeing with a Kingdom reality. Most of us have not come to this place about ownership.

## Liberty Is the Atmosphere of the Kingdom

Yet this kind of understanding is liberating, and liberty is the atmosphere of the Kingdom. It will enable you to live in God's peace, and peace is a promise of the Kingdom. You don't lie awake at night worrying about protecting something that does not belong to you. You don't get ulcers over an untenable situation at work if you have given the Lord the responsibility for your future. You won't worry about whether or not you will get "that job" or "that promotion" or "that business deal" because you are one of His bondservants and the bondservant has chosen to place his life in the hands of his Master.

If you agree with the Lord on the issue of ownership, then He is responsible for these things. We must do our part and be responsible stewards of all these things, but the control that comes with ownership is His. To put it another way, we are responsible for effort, integrity, study, knowledge, and stewardship; He is responsible for outcomes. This way of living is diametrically opposed to the systems of this world.

The Kingdom perspective is entirely different! Everything we have belongs to Him. This extends not only to your possessions or lack of them, but your business, your future, your calling, and your family. If we are going to live in this Kingdom Economy, we must learn to live in contentment, with expectation.

# If He Owns It, He Controls the Outcome

If you are a business leader, manager, or owner, your business belongs to Him. To put this in very practical terms, if it is His business, then He is responsible to cause the business to flourish. We are to work very hard and very smart, educate ourselves, understand the times, and do all we can to be wise stewards of God's business, but the responsibility for the business is His. This may sound ethereal and mystical, but the reality of this has very practical applications.

## Surrender

Surrendering is giving to the Lord what we may at one time have viewed as our own. I learned there are levels of this kind of surrender. After I gave my business to the Lord, I would periodically go to the office before anyone arrived for work to pray over the office. I would lay hands on the checking accounts, pray over each of the offices and each employee, and pray for unity in my staff and for the peace of God to reign while I worshiped the Lord. Years after I had dedicated the business to God, I went to my office early one morning to pray. This particular morning the Lord said to me, "Son, you need to give Me the business."

I was surprised by this and said, "Lord, I have given You this business many times. I am not aware of anything I have retained ownership of, but if You want me to surrender it to You again, I will. Lord, I give You this business on a deeper level than I have ever done before. All of it is Yours, what I'm conscious of and what I'm not conscious of."

Suddenly, at 6:15 in the morning, the presence of God flooded that place. That morning changed my perspective on the issue of ownership. In a very practical way, I began to understand the responsibilities that come with ownership and those that come with stewardship. God seems to require a progressive surrender with things like this.

## HIRING PROCEDURES

If we are in fact stewards of God's business, then He has the right to make decisions concerning His business. We sometimes make wrong decisions because we do not do what James 1:5 says, *"But if any of you lacks wisdom, let him ask of God, who gives to all generously and without reproach, and it will be given to him."*

There are many practical ways to approach this. One way to hire people is to write the job description and personality profile you want for that position, set it before the Lord, and say, "Lord, I think this is who we need to hire for Your business. Will You send this person to us so we don't have to interview hundreds of people and depend on our own judgment to fill this position?" Praying for key hires is important. You may think, *This won't work for me. You are living in a dream world!* I will say to you, this is not an original idea!

Luke 6:12-13 says:

*It was at this time that He went off to the mountain to pray, and He spent the whole night in prayer to God. And when day came, He called His disciples to Him and chose twelve of them, whom He also named…*

Jesus had many followers at this time, but He knew the time had come to make some personnel decisions. He needed His senior management team, so to speak, and He had 12 openings. Jesus did not interview, He appointed. These 12 men would be His legacy, and they would manage what would become the largest, most dynamic organization in the history of the world—the Body of Christ.

Let's remember who was making the decision on these 12 senior-level people: none other than Jesus Christ, the Son of God, about whom Colossians 2:3 says, *"In whom are hidden all the treasures of wisdom and knowledge."*

All the treasures of wisdom and knowledge were in Jesus, and He realized He needed to spend the night alone in prayer to get God the Father's ideas on these 12 appointments. Then who are we to flippantly make key personnel decisions about God's businesses without consulting with the real Owner? If He owns it, He gets to decide who works in His business. He is a much better judge of character than I am, since He knows the thoughts and intents of the heart (see Heb. 4:12 NKJV).

On some level, every Kingdom business can adopt this principle. You may have a variation on the theme outlined here, but include Him in your decisions. You have at your disposal the wisdom of God. Why not use His wisdom? If you are a CEO of a multi-national corporation, use this for your key leaders. If you run a small business, use it for all your hires.

## GIVE HIM HIS PLACE

When I had staff meetings, I would set a chair at the head of the table for the Lord and invite Him to take His place. This was not some superficial approach to doing things. The Lord was invited to sit with us and participate with His wisdom. There are many ways you can acknowledge and honor Him in business without beating people over the head with your Bible. Ask Him to show you. He is already involved in your business. Why not acknowledge His involvement by making a place for Him?

## LET GOD STAY AWAKE— YOU GO TO SLEEP

In the early years of my business, we were going through a difficult time, and I had a cash flow problem. I had given the business to the Lord over and over again, so ownership was not an issue. My understanding of how that ownership worked operationally was the issue.

One of my key people was a young man with four young children. One night I could not sleep because I was worried about making payroll in a few days. I kept thinking about George's children, and I just didn't see how everything was going to work. I tossed and turned until about 2:00 A.M. when suddenly, another layer of the understanding about God's ownership came to light.

I sat up in bed and said, "Wait a minute! If this is Your business, why am I lying awake worrying about how to make payroll for Your business? Psalm 121:4 says You *"…neither slumber nor sleep."* Lord, You can be thinking about how to make Your payroll, because I'm going to sleep." I went to sleep, and God did make His payroll. I have never lost a minute's sleep over those kinds of issues since.

## THE GRIEVING PERIOD

Once again, if He owns it, then we are essentially stewards of Another's resources. The dictionary defines a *steward* in this way: "one who manages another's property, finances, or other affairs; an administrator; supervisor."[1] In other words, we carry the responsibility to use the resources the way they are intended to be used.

Stewardship also means short grieving periods. When you lose "the deal" that you have clothed in integrity, prayer, and effort, allow yourself five minutes of grief and move on. One godly businessman told me, "When God hands you a business deal, the issue then becomes our stewardship of that deal because He owns it. If He owns it, then He can cause that deal to flourish and be very profitable or He can cause it to die."

God does not need "the deal" to keep His businesses going because His businesses have no such needs. His businesses are fully supplied for His purposes because they are part of His Kingdom and they function by the standards of His Kingdom's Economy. His Kingdom does not operate on the basis of need. It operates from a position of full supply.

These are some very practical aspects regarding ownership and operating in the Kingdom Economy. Because we are only stewards of what we have been given, we are accountable to the Lord for the proper use of His resources. We are responsible to Him for the use of not only His silver and His gold, but of our time and all the elements of our life in the marketplace. Jesus illustrated this in the parable of the talents (see Matt. 25:14-30).

In a previous chapter, we discussed the two kingdoms being expressed in different worldviews and having distinct characteristics and perspectives on any given issue. Ownership is a critical one of those perspectives. Let's look at some practical, tangible considerations that will help us understand the Economy of the Kingdom.

In order for the economic element of the Kingdom to come to fulfillment in our lives, a transformation in our thinking and understanding must first take place. As His people, we have the responsibility of knowing how God's system of economics works. What is our viewpoint to be? How do we succeed in His Economy? How does God define success?

These are questions many of us should begin asking as we draw near to the coming of the Lord. We live in a day when the revelation of these things is upon us. Responsibly representing the Lord's desires with His resources is a very serious matter. The Lord is preparing to pour out great resources upon nations, businesses, and individuals, and we must come to understand the breadth of the Kingdom Economy in order to understand our roles.

# FINANCIAL RESOURCE AS A RESPONSIBILITY

For many of us, our understanding of the Kingdom Economy is limited to giving and receiving and tithes and offerings. Since the culture of the Kingdom is one of generosity, these two elements are essential. Malachi 3:10 says:

> *"Bring the whole tithe into the storehouse, so that there may be food in My house, and test Me now in this,"* *says the LORD of hosts, "if I will not open for you the windows of heaven and pour out for you a blessing until it overflows."*

Most of us around the world who sit in the pews on Sunday morning have heard expositions of this verse many times. It is absolute truth. All those who have understood this truth have been personally blessed by this verse, because the Kingdom Economy does include giving and receiving. It does include paying of tithes and giving of offerings. These things are an essential part of living in the Kingdom Economy. However, God's economic system is much broader in scope than just those two elements.

The Kingdom perspective is that we are responsible, as stewards, to the real Owner of everything, and that includes finances. The question always becomes: How does God want me to spend His money? Tithes and offerings are part of this culture of generosity that exists in the Kingdom. We have been given the role of financing the work of God around the world. It is appropriate that people in the marketplace finance the crusades, the ministries, and the missionaries with God's money.

## Penetrating Questions

However, is it not possible that God's money should also go toward building roads so small farmers in developing countries can get their products to market? Who will supply the capital and wise counsel for the godly owner of the cash-starved manufacturing firm in Brazil that employs 200 people (200 families)? Who will finance building deep wells in villages all over Africa so little children don't die because of disease?

How can we help the poor in developing nations learn the biblical principles of entrepreneurship so they can sustain themselves? These are penetrating questions that need to be asked if we are to flourish in the Kingdom Economy because the Kingdom is about community responsibility.

I will grant you that building roads is not as "flashy" as some of the things the Body of Christ does with God's money. We may not become a "ministry friend" for providing counsel and low interest capital to the manufacturing facility. We probably don't make the Christian television or radio talk show circuit as superstar businesspeople for drilling wells in Africa. But the question is, "How does God want His money invested?"

Does God only want His money invested on Wall Street or the Tokyo Stock Exchange? Please understand there is absolutely nothing wrong with doing this as part of a Spirit-led strategy. However, I think He looks at "return on investment" differently. Is He going to say, "Well done, thou good and faithful servant! You got a thirty percent annualized return over a ten-year period on My money!" Or is He going to say, "You took that return and started a self-funding foundation to fund orphanages in South America. Well done!" We are responsible to "invest" His money where we can get His kind of return.

I submit these questions to you as one who has asked them. These questions may be uncomfortable to answer, but they need to be asked. The Economy of the Kingdom is a comprehensive, dynamic part of the Kingdom of God that Jesus preached about. It affects the spiritual side of life, but it also produces tangible benefits to small businesses, large corporations, employees, and employers. It impacts government leadership, as well as our homes and families.

This Economy does include Malachi 3:10, but it is not limited to that verse. The Kingdom Economy includes every verse in Scripture. God gave us His plan for a comprehensive lifestyle within His Kingdom. It is a practical, all-encompassing way of living that affects every area of our lives, including personal stewardship.

# Responsibility of "Hidden Treasures"

Several godly political leaders in high positions of government have told me privately that the Lord has said He will reveal "hidden treasures" in their nations when righteous government leadership is in place. One of these men is a key government leader in a nation that is very poor, with 70 percent unemployment. Make no mistake: God controls the natural resources and their discovery.

God desires righteous government and business leadership in place for this kind of thing so the benefit goes to the people of the nation, not to a corrupt few. This kind of thing happens when there is a partnership of government and business. Righteous leaders understand the principle of ownership and responsibility and won't use God-given resource for personal gain at the expense of those God wants to bless.

## FINANCIAL RESOURCE AS A REWARD

In the economic system of the world, resource is often viewed as a reward for personal achievement, brilliance, or human effort. According to this view, a reward brings little or no accountability. It can be spent on personal desires as you wish. You "own" the reward, and you are responsible only to yourself. You have no community responsibility to bless others with what you have.

In some developing nations, the resources are often controlled by a small group of business and government leaders who consider maintenance of the status quo and consolidation of their wealth as primary goals. The resources are managed at the expense of the poor, and many times this lays the foundation for political unrest and discontent. If we operate in this system, we will never have enough.

In the world's economic system, no matter how much you accumulate, you will never be satisfied with what you have. Proverbs 27:20 (NKJV) says, *"…So the eyes of man are never satisfied."*

In this economic system, the reality of the Lord as the *Jehovah Jireh* (the "Provider") is constantly called into question. This system is based on lack and need that you may perceive in your life. We become envious of what others have, and therefore doubt God's ability to provide for His people. God's ability and desire to provide for His people are part of His character. When we doubt His ability or His desire to provide for us, we doubt His character.

## Supernatural Versus Natural

The Kingdom Economy operates supernaturally. Therefore faith, our complete trust in Him, is a central component. Hebrews 11:6 says:

> *And without faith it is impossible to please Him, for he who comes to God must believe that He is and that He is a rewarder of those who seek Him.*

Believing that He is fully engaged in all aspects of our lives, including our businesses, is the beginning of *"believing that He is."* He operates on a different plane than we do. God has absolutely no limitations on what He can do in our lives, except the limitations we put on Him. He can't do more because He has already done everything.

The economic system of the world can only operate on a natural basis. This system depends solely on you to produce. When you can't produce, you are of no value. This is a one-dimensional system with limitations.

## GOD'S DIRECTION

In Genesis 26, we are told that Isaac was living in a foreign land in a time of famine. The implication of the Hebrew word for famine is "by Jehovah's word." I am not, by any means, suggesting that all famine is caused by God. But I am saying that in this case it appears to be so.

Isaac knew he could not control the external circumstances in his life and business. He had many servants (employees) and large herds and needed to feed them. He was directed to a nation and a people who were hostile to him on land he didn't even own. He was a renter, so to speak. He had to gain permission from the king of the Philistines to stay there. Genesis 26:12-13 says:

> *Now Isaac sowed in that land and reaped in the same year a hundredfold. And the LORD blessed him, and the man became rich, and continued to grow richer until he became very wealthy.*

## PHYSICAL IMPOSSIBILITIES DON'T CHALLENGE GOD'S POWER

I spoke about this verse to an agricultural engineer while I was holding a MarketPlace Leadership Conference in El Salvador. Melina told me, "What took place here was a physical impossibility; it cannot happen in the natural."

We have to understand that God's power was not challenged in making this happen. His methods are beyond natural means; they are supernatural. Isaac sowed the seed in one season, and in that same season his harvest yielded a 10,000 percent return on investment.

This was supernatural and produced a fear of Isaac's God in the heart of the king of Philistia and his people. This supernatural event and others caused the Philistine leaders to have a new respect for Isaac. God did this because He loved Isaac, but more importantly because He was working within His strategic plan for the nations of the earth.

We have to understand that the economic system of the Kingdom operates supernaturally. When you have surrendered ownership, find the mind of the Lord in your work life, pray according to His will, and ask Him to bring it to pass because you are unable to do so. Trust that He will do it, declare it with your lips, let your efforts equal your prayers and declarations, and thank Him. Then wait expectantly for the answer, no matter how long it takes.

## DIVINELY POSITIONED

It is clear that the Lord is setting things in order in our day. When we come into agreement with God on this issue of ownership, we begin to move ourselves into the position where we can be useful to the Kingdom—we become trustworthy, or worthy of God's trust.

We can then use God's resources the way He intends them to be used. We can do what it says in Malachi 3:10 and *"bring the whole tithe into the storehouse,"* but we can also impact our nations for the Kingdom by being fathers to the fatherless. We can help the widows and orphans, clothe the naked, heal the sick. We can become righteous business leaders who use God's resources to care for our employees and government leaders who use our God-given influence for righteousness—not personal gain.

In order to handle the resources of God, our hands must be clean and our hearts determined to fulfill the Kingdom work that we have been uniquely equipped to do. The Lord will teach us how to operate in the Kingdom Economy once we understand this basic premise of ownership.

ENDNOTE

1. *The American Heritage Dictionary of the English Language* (New York: American Heritage Publishing Co., Inc, 1969, 1970), 1265.

# CHAPTER 5

## *Questions for Consideration*

1. Do you become uncomfortable when discussing the issue of God's ownership?

_____

_____

_____

_____

_____

_____

2. Do you embrace tithing as mentioned in Malachi 3:10, or are you afraid you won't have enough?

_____

_____

_____

3.  Do you consider yourself an owner or a steward of the important things in your life? Describe what you do to express that viewpoint.

_____

_____

_____

_____

_____

_____

_____

_____

_____

_____

4.  How could the reality of the Kingdom Economy being a supernatural economy impact you personally?

_____

_____

_____

_____

_____

_____

_____

_____

5. Do you consider the resources you have as a responsibility you must steward, or a reward you have no accountability for?

_____

_____

_____

_____

_____

_____

_____

_____

# CHAPTER 6

## *Revelation Supersedes Calculation*

*At that time the L*ORD *said to Joshua, "Make for yourself flint knives and circumcise again the sons of Israel the second time." So Joshua made himself flint knives and circumcised the sons of Israel at Gibeath-haaraloth* (Joshua 5:2-3).

I have often considered the absurdity of these verses when put in the context of the events taking place at that time. After "wandering" around in the desert for 40 years under the leadership of Moses, the Israelites crossed the Jordan River under a new leader, Joshua. They marched to a place where the high walls of the impregnable city of Jericho were visible to the sons and daughters of Israel.

Young warriors must have been sharpening their swords, their palms sweaty with the anticipation of their first battle in this new land of promise. Their leaders were likely gathered together planning the strategy of the attack.

Though the Bible does not say, it is reasonable to assume that Joshua, a man who was trained and mentored by "the friend of God," Moses, was alone seeking the Lord over the challenge that was set before him. In challenging times he was trained to go to the tent of meeting.

Any great leader cares for the well-being of those he leads, and Joshua was no different. In order for him to be God's appointed leader, Joshua had to exhibit the same care and concern that the Lord had for His people. The Lord's plan for the "assault" on Jericho had not yet been revealed, so this was a time of uncertainty. Since Joshua was a military commander and the leader of God's people, it is likely he was considering the cost in lives to make this first conquest in the Promised Land.

True Kingdom leaders, whether they are military commanders, government leaders, ministry heads, or middle managers in a corporate setting, have to position themselves to receive instruction and direction from their King. In times of crisis, God always has a plan that will produce success, as He defines success. He is never without a plan for any situation!

Real leadership in His Kingdom means that leaders oftentimes have to sequester themselves away from the many distractions of life and listen. When we do this, we find the wisdom and the strategies of God will be revealed to us.

One such leader who understood this principle was John Wesley, the founder of the Methodist movement. Historians credit Wesley with having a significant, transforming effect on the moral and cultural decay that was taking place in Great Britain in the 1700s. He was a man used by God to bring His transforming power to the people of a nation that was in decline. These transformed people, in turn, influenced the cultural fabric of the nation—the family, business, government, and ministry. Yet where did one man get these special qualities necessary to produce change like that?

## Divine Visitations

John Wesley would spend from 4:00 A.M. to 8:00 A.M. every day alone in quiet communion with God, worship, prayer, and study of His Word. Wesley said:

> Those that desire communion with God must keep their spirits quiet and serene. All hurry of spirit and turbulent passions make us unfit for divine visitations.[1]

The power to transform, not only our personal lives but organizations and nations, awaits us in the quiet place. Like Wesley, we can position ourselves for these "divine visitations"!

## Obedient and Committed Leaders

While the soldiers of Jericho were taunting the Israelite intruders from the parapet walls, the Lord spoke to His general and said, "Circumcise your army." This command of the Lord incapacitated the army for days and seemingly placed in jeopardy the women and children of the entire nation. It is also safe to assume that Joshua's "revelation" was probably not enthusiastically received by his leaders and those who were about to be circumcised, to say nothing of the rest of the population of the nation. A quick "calculation" of the pros and cons would have provided some obvious conclusions.

However, the obedience and commitment of God's appointed leader in the face of opposition produced an astonishing result. Joshua 5:9 says:

*Then the LORD said to Joshua, "Today I have rolled away the reproach of Egypt from you." So the name of that place is called Gilgal to this day.*

The very day the nation was circumcised, God removed the reproach, the taunts, the mockery, and the contempt of the Egyptians and the surrounding nations.

God's people had been viewed as irrelevant, an object of scorn and disdain by the surrounding nations because of what appeared to be aimless wandering in the desert for 40 years. The Jews had no "king" like other nations. During those 40 years, they did not have land to call their own; they did not have farms and herds like everyone else. The Jews gave the appearance of an aimless group of nomads, somehow surviving in the desert by some mysterious sustenance that floated down from Heaven. Certainly this group of wanderers could not be a threat to anyone.

The "wandering" will always seem aimless to the scoffer. Sometimes it seems pointless to us, but God is always strategic in everything He does. If He has set you on a course, stay the course until He changes the course. Because of Joshua's obedience to this difficult command, God supernaturally removed this reproach from the entire nation, and the scorned now became the feared. It was not the victory at Jericho that caused the reproach to be rolled away; it was the circumcision before Jericho!

## REVELATION SUPERSEDES CALCULATION

In the Kingdom Economy, "revelation" supersedes our "calculation." Revelation does not eliminate the need for calculation, but when revelation comes, it takes the primary position in the decision-making process. In Joshua's case, the "revelation" was absurd and beyond the boundaries of reason. It is important to understand what took place here. Joshua didn't circumcise because he thought God might be pleased. He positioned himself to hear the Lord at a critical time, and when God spoke, he obeyed a difficult command in the face of opposition. Joshua responded to what God said; he didn't ask God to respond to what he did.

In this Kingdom Economy, God's people will flourish in the days ahead by positioning themselves to hear the Lord and responding to His voice. He is preparing His people for a time when His Economy will be the dominant economy on the earth. There will be tribulation and challenges, but if we are to thrive, we will need His revelation to function.

# ECONOMIC DOWNTURNS ARE IRRELEVANT TO THE KINGDOM

Remember, the Kingdom Economy operates on a supernatural basis, so it is never susceptible to economic downturns. It is not supernatural for God's people to prosper in good times because everyone can do that. For God's people to prosper when there are economic challenges everywhere is supernatural and that is where the Lord wants to bring His people. That is exactly how the Kingdom operates, and that is also how we function in the Kingdom Economy.

I am not suggesting that good judgment, a high degree of organization, strategic planning, and excellence are not necessary in this Kingdom Economy. On the contrary, an even greater commitment to these things is required because in this economic system we represent the Lord in all things. When we choose to live in the Economy of the Kingdom, we conduct affairs with the Lord's involvement in our daily work life. Because this economic system functions by supernatural means, revelation is available—and in fact expected.

When we choose to operate by His principles, we are more able to control outcomes rather than being victims of outcomes that others control. We can do this because we operate under His authority and we have been given permission to use that authority.

It is possible, and even expected, to manage people by the principles of the Bible. Leaders can lead, managers can manage, and workers can work by the precepts of Scripture. This is living in the Economy of the Kingdom.

You can expect to make investments by the voice of the Holy Spirit. You will make mistakes, but it won't be because God's knowledge of the investment is flawed, it will be because you didn't listen well enough or execute the timing necessary. Are you thinking this is too much? I've met people all over the globe who are doing this! So it's too late to tell me it's too much.

We serve an all-knowing God who has known everything from before the beginning of time. If you are going to invest money based on a future return, whose knowledge of the future would you trust more—yours or God's? As we live our lives before Him in righteousness and holiness, as we honor the Lord and bring Him honor in all our dealings, and as we position ourselves to listen to Him, we will open ourselves up to the wisdom of God in everything.

Let me be very clear here: the Lord has no obligation to bless sloppy business practices just because we are believers. You can tithe and give offerings and go to church every time the doors are open, but if you lack integrity, if you do not pay your suppliers, if you oppress the wage earner who is in your employ, if you lack good judgment and planning, you will fail.

If you are an employee and you do not give your employer an honest day's labor, you are not honoring God with your work. *The grace of God covers many things, but it will not cover a lack of integrity in your business dealings and your treatment of people.*

Of all people on the earth, God's people should have the best-run businesses and operate in the highest standards of integrity because we represent Jesus to the world. A well-run, organized business can reach nations for the Gospel that are currently closed to missionaries. A poorly run business that lacks integrity brings reproach on us and the name of the Lord. Colossians 3:23-24 says:

> *Whatever you do, do your work heartily, as for the Lord rather than for men, knowing that from the Lord you will receive the reward of the inheritance. It is the Lord Christ whom you serve.*

We are to live in His Kingdom, not try to make Him live in ours.

God told Moses in Exodus 31:6, *"...in the hearts of all who are skillful I have put skill...."* You carry the gifts and talents you have because God has given them to you. The word *sanctify* in Scripture means "to make holy, to purify, to consecrate, render, or declare sacred or holy; to separate from things profane and dedicate to God."[2] This definition implies action on the part of the one doing the sanctifying. This is the day for us to sanctify these gifts and talents for His use.

## UNUSUAL GIFTS?

I have a friend named John who was founder and chairman of the board of an emerging bank. John said, "God has given me a gift to start banks." This is a "gift" that will probably not be spoken about from pulpits on Sunday morning. It does not fit in the discussion about the "five-fold ministry" gifts (see Eph. 4:11-13). Yet this is a unique gift, given by the Lord for a specific purpose for His Kingdom.

Some of you have a unique gifting for a specific purpose. You may not even recognize it as a gift from God. Yet God told Moses, and He is telling us today, *"In the hearts of all who are skillful I have put skill" (Exod. 31:6).*

John said he clearly heard the voice of the Lord speak one day to start a new bank based strictly on Kingdom principles. The Lord said the bank was to issue business loans by the direction of the Holy Spirit *(revelation)* and not necessarily by standard banking practices that determine financial strength *(calculation)*. The loan committee laid hands on the loan applications, prayed, and waited for the Holy Spirit to direct. Many times they gave loans that did not make sense by standard banking practice. Yet each time they tried to follow the leading of the Spirit. They provided funding for churches when other banks would not do so. Always this would be by the leading of the Holy Spirit.

I am not suggesting that John's bank ignored sound banking practice. They were thorough in their preparation and evaluation and did not loan money to everyone. Nor did they loan money to every church or every Christian with a business idea. They were led by the Holy Spirit first and the use of sound banking principles second.

John was putting at risk the money of those who trusted him with their investment capital, and he took this responsibility very seriously. The bank started very small, yet it grew rapidly. Today this bank is a significant force in the home mortgage business in our region, and John is off starting another bank.

In the Kingdom Economy, we have an obligation for thorough calculation because we work as His representative *"as for the Lord rather than men."* Once again, however, "revelation" supersedes "calculation."

## Conflicting Economies

In a worldly economic system, calculation—what makes sense to the natural intellect, what shows on a balance sheet or a profit and loss statement—is the sole standard of measurement. Decisions are made and value assigned based on what is known, seen, and felt: the senses. Making a profit can be more important than the way you make the profit: the process.

In the Kingdom, the process by which the profit is made is more important than the profit. Profitability is the goal of every business, and Kingdom business is not different. God expects us to be profitable and He can show us how to be more profitable. However, as His representatives, He expects us to honor commitments and to fully execute agreements with our clients even when it costs us to do so. I learned that in the Kingdom when the process pleases God, the profit will follow.

Revelation will always be viewed with skepticism, suspicion, and mockery in a worldly economic system. As we saw earlier, the world's system is driven by the demonic force Jesus spoke of called "mammon" (confidence in wealth or power; the spirit of avarice or greed). Jesus told us this system is in direct opposition to anything that God endorses. He said in Luke 16:13 (NKJV):

*No servant can serve two masters; for either he will hate the one and love the other, or else he will be loyal to the one and despise the other. You cannot serve God and mammon.*

Both require service, but it is impossible to serve both. When we serve God we serve Him as a bondservant, a willing servant. When we serve mammon we are driven by it. We must choose which one to serve.

## PROSPERITY TO FACILITATE THE KINGDOM

It is good for us to remember that the Father sent His Son for people, not for prosperity. Prosperity is a by-product that comes with a purpose. This Kingdom Economy is being established to facilitate the redemption of humankind through the coming of His Son. God is beginning to release financial resource in the hands of those He can trust. We will be entrusted with varying degrees of financial resource because of God's sovereignty. Those with fewer resources do not need to feel guilty or unworthy, and they should not envy those with more.

Some are called to fund the "witty inventions" of the Lord—last-days, for-profit businesses that will generate great income for Kingdom strategies. Some men and women have the calling of "paymasters" for the Kingdom. I know individuals who have told me they know this is their "call." These last-days marketplace leaders live in every nation. They quietly sit in congregations around the world.

Once again, these men and women will rarely ever stand up on Sunday morning and testify about this calling. They quietly go about their work with no fanfare because their fulfillment comes from carrying out their roles and pleasing the Lord, not from the accolades of people. These men and women have been tested and proved faithful. They can be trusted with God's resources; therefore He will give them *His vision for His resources.*

Some have experienced this increase, while some are in the testing process. One thing is certain: God will use a sanctified marketplace to fund His last-days strategies. We must get ready for our place and exercise these sanctified gifts for the sanctified markets of the Kingdom Economy. His gifts, for His purposes, for His Kingdom!

ENDNOTES

1.  John Wesley, *John Wesley's Notes on the Whole Bible, The Old Testament* (Albany, OR: SAGE Software, 1996), 1092.

2.  Strong, *A Concise Dictionary of the Words in the Hebrew Bible*, 102.

# CHAPTER 6

## *Questions for Consideration*

1. When was the last time you had one of those "divine visitations" Wesley spoke about?

_____

_____

_____

_____

_____

_____

2. Do you position yourself every day to receive the Lord's direction?

_____

_____

_____

3. Have you ever had the Lord speak to you about something (revelation), and after thorough evaluation (calculation) reluctantly obeyed and found out He was right?

---

4. You have something that you are really good at. Have you ever considered that according to Exodus 31:6, God may have given you that skill?

---

5. If you are a steward, would you ask God right now to give you a vision for His resources and your life?

_____

_____

_____

_____

_____

_____

_____

_____

# CHAPTER 7

## *God's Leaders Are Revealed in Times of Crisis*

*Then I said to them, "You see the bad situation we are in, that Jerusalem is desolate and its gates burned by fire. Come, let us rebuild the wall of Jerusalem so that we will no longer be a reproach." I told them how the hand of my God had been favorable to me and also about the king's words which he had spoken to me. Then they said, "Let us arise and build." So they put their hands to the good work* (Nehemiah 2:17-18).

We live in the days spoken about in Matthew 24:8 (NKJV) *"...these are the beginning of sorrows."* This shaking is upon us. Institutions that we have long relied upon are shaking; large international businesses are crumbling; governments are being torn down and built up; and people are polarized politically and religiously. In addition, we are seeing unprecedented natural phenomena, wars and rumors of wars, and corruption being exposed on all levels.

Many nations exist on the edge of crisis, and the solutions offered by business, government, and religious leaders don't seem to match the problems. Leadership seems to be failing us. Could it be that the eyes of the world are beginning to look upward?

## LEADERS REVEALED IN CRISIS

In a previous chapter, I defined the leader who is anointed and inspired. Implementing God's strategies during times of crisis requires this kind of leadership. The Book of Nehemiah is a textbook example of the type of godly leadership needed in most nations at the present time. Leadership is the answer today, just as it was in Nehemiah's time.

In many nations the Lord is establishing leaders like Nehemiah. They are empowered to establish the culture of the Kingdom where they live and work every day. These men and women are God's agents of cultural transformation. They have been anointed to lead in business, ministry, medicine, government, education, justice, media, and finance. They are gifted people who have been tested, and they are appointed to lead us through these difficult times.

Crisis will always betray bad leadership or reveal good leadership. Some of these anointed leaders are obvious to us today. However, some have not yet stepped into their role of leadership. How do we identify the men and women who will lead this transformation? What are their characteristics and how do we help facilitate them to do what they are appointed to do?

Just as times and seasons change, the nature of crisis also changes. However, the model for God's leadership remains a constant. Throughout Scripture the Lord has given us many representations of leadership during difficult times. Nehemiah remains one such model of leadership in critical times. How could a man who lived thousands of years ago be relevant today? Nehemiah himself wrote the book that bears his name, so we are getting a first-person report of the process of accepting the assignment and the subsequent challenges for him in a time of real crisis. Though circumstances may change, the challenges to the Kingdom priorities have remained a constant.

## LEADERS WHO PRAY

In the text Nehemiah had arrived in a Jerusalem that had been totally destroyed by Nebuchadnezzar 142 years earlier. While most Jews had been carried into exile, a remnant had remained. Without walls to protect the city, they were subject to the violence and oppression of neighbors hostile to God's people. Josephus, the Jewish historian, said of Jerusalem and this remnant prior to Nehemiah's arrival:

> ...they were in a bad state for that their walls were thrown down to the ground, and that the neighboring nations did a great deal of mischief to the Jews, while in the daytime they overran the country, and pillaged it, and in the night did

them mischief, insomuch that not a few were led away captive out of the country, and out of Jerusalem itself, and that the roads were in the daytime found full of dead men.[1]

This was not a pretty picture for Nehemiah's countrymen, yet it is not unlike some nations in the world today. In most developing nations the poor live in survival mode and suffer daily oppression.

Nehemiah was living in Susa, the capital of Persia, when he heard the report of his people. He was the cupbearer to the king of Persia. His response to the report about the Jewish people is found in Nehemiah 1:4-6:

*...I sat down and wept and mourned for days; and I was fasting and praying before the God of heaven. I said, "I beseech You, O LORD God of heaven, the great and awesome God, who preserves the covenant and lovingkindness for those who love Him and keep His commandments, let Your ear now be attentive and Your eyes open to hear the prayer of Your servant which I am praying before You now, day and night, on behalf of the sons of Israel Your servants...."*

Many people in the marketplace are people of action. We sometimes have the opinion that great things can be accomplished because of great leadership. While this is certainly true on some levels, the challenges of today that require Kingdom leadership call for more than that. For Nehemiah, the assignment began with intercession. Inspired, anointed leaders—and that is exactly what it will take in our day—begin assignments on their knees.

My friend Jan Christie, a woman who is an intercessor and a teacher of intercessors, says, "The things you walk out in life as one of God's leaders have already been obtained for you by prayer and intercession."

Men and women with a commission for this kind of leadership, one that represents the will of the Lord for others, will be people of action who have a life of prayer and an understanding of intercession. Nehemiah was willing to lay the foundation for his action by carrying a burden in prayer for a people and a nation. Today's leaders are no different because this is God's way for success. Success can come no other way.

## GOD EMPOWERS AFTER ACCEPTANCE

Most likely Nehemiah lived a comfortable life in the capital city of Susa. In his position, it would be reasonable to assume that the king of Persia, the ruler of the most powerful nation on earth at the time, would pay him well to keep him from being susceptible to a bribe. Otherwise, the king would subject himself to the risk of poisoning. However, in the annals of history you will not find many cupbearers mentioned as playing a key role in events of their day. The reason is that cupbearers were not policy makers. Cupbearers didn't make decisions that would impact nations. They didn't lead great armies into battle.

Nehemiah was the exception. He was an unlikely candidate to lead the transformation of the most important city on earth, yet he was the one who accepted the assignment. Once he accepted the assignment, he was empowered to fulfill the task.

Nehemiah served the king of Persia as a trusted and important servant. He grew up as an exile in Persia who had likely never seen Jerusalem. Jerusalem was a dangerous, 900-mile journey across hostile territory. In his day, such journeys were not frequent. Why would Nehemiah care about a people 900 miles away when he was a comfortable, high-profile servant of the king of the most powerful nation on earth? By any worldly standard, Nehemiah had no reason to leave the comfort of Susa and take up this burden for a people who were 900 miles away in a city he had probably never seen. It was not a reasonable decision to make.

Yet, in Nehemiah 1:4-11, we see the foundations for the wall of Jerusalem being laid through fasting, prayer, and intercession for the people. One city has always been foremost in the mind of every Jew, and that city is Jerusalem. It has been, and continues to be, the city around which the history of the world revolves. Nehemiah was experiencing the same burden God had for the people. This kind of burden for the welfare of a people is simply accepted, not self-generated. Out of this season of prayer, he asked the Lord to empower him to become the solution.

## WAS NEHEMIAH THE FIRST?

God's priorities revolve around His greatest treasure—people. Jesus left His throne in Heaven to liberate this treasure. God sent Nehemiah to Jerusalem for the sake of people who were defenseless against oppressors. The overriding message in the Book of Nehemiah isn't the wall; it is the protection of God's greatest treasure. Nehemiah was not sent to Jerusalem with God's authorization to inspire others to work on a construction project. Ultimately God doesn't care about buildings, political parties, organizations, businesses, denominations, or governments. He cares about the people involved in them and the people affected by them.

Before Nehemiah, how many people had God begun to speak to about His concern for Jerusalem and her people? How many may have said, "I'm too comfortable. It is too risky. I go to synagogue every Sabbath and that's enough." I often wonder if Nehemiah was the first person God spoke to about this task. I can assure you God is looking for Nehemiahs today who are willing to take up positions of leadership in cities and nations and bring about a Kingdom transformation to benefit people.

Some of these leaders may have a life of comfort. They may be influencers in their cities or in the marketplace. They may be people who have attained some success, or they may be obscure men and women who have been faithful to the tasks set before them but are yet waiting for their leadership assignment. I know many of these leaders who know the assignment is coming, but they may not know what form it will take or how it will be accomplished. I have discovered that God likes to require extended times of preparation for this kind of leader. They never develop overnight. When a person has an assignment to this kind of leadership, God will always provide tests of faithfulness, integrity, and personal holiness along the way to ensure that the vessel is worthy to contain the precious oil that will come from Heaven.

These individuals must have a fire that burns inside them in order for the impossible to take place, for a people to become free, for the status quo to change, and for the Kingdom to be established. Just as with Nehemiah, God's concerns will become their concerns during their quiet times with the Lord, when the only audience is Heaven. These leaders will first cry out for a people or a nation alone before the Lord. In these quiet times they take on the desires of the Father for His people. Once this happens, the walls of the city will be built! *At the point of acceptance the concept becomes a reality.*

We must, however, take it one step further. We have to make a "covenant with the vision" God has given. At this point, life takes on new meaning. We have eliminated the options for any other life, and a single focus comes into view to use our unique gifts to serve this purpose of His Kingdom. At the end of the first chapter when Nehemiah makes this "covenant," God's plan for Jerusalem becomes his plan also.

## GIFTED AND INSPIRED LEADERSHIP

Gifted leadership is not uncommon. Gifted and inspired leaders with a heart like Nehemiah are the only ones who implement a transformed culture of a nation, business, or government. Leaders with a decision-making capacity inspired by the Holy Spirit through times of prayer and intercession are those God can trust to represent His purposes. When you know how to find the will of God through prayer, you will have Heaven's support for your efforts because your efforts are initiated on your knees.

These marketplace leaders are people with a purpose beyond their occupations. They are government leaders with a desire to end corruption so the blessing of God can come upon their nation. They are physicians with a passion for medical care for the poor. They are gifted financiers with a consuming desire to use what God is giving them to change cities or nations. They are barristers and lawyers who desire true justice for all people regardless of their economic positions. They are media people who want to use this powerful weapon of culture to establish righteousness rather than just to entertain. The common thread woven through the life of these leaders is a commitment to seek God.

## Risk Takers!

To be sad in the presence of the king was an offense punishable by death. Nehemiah risked his life if he entered into the presence of the king with anything but a smile. Yet carrying this burden for his people for four months was revealed on his countenance.

> *So the king said to me, "Why is your face sad though you are not sick? This is nothing but sadness of heart." Then I was very much afraid. I said to the king, "Let the king live forever. Why should my face not be sad when the city, the place of my fathers' tombs, lies desolate and its gates have been consumed by fire?"* (Nehemiah 2:2-3)

Nehemiahs are risk takers. These leaders see the impossible as a completed work. They will do what is unpopular; they will go where it is not comfortable; and they will commit to a work when everyone is telling them they are foolish. These are the people Daniel spoke of in Daniel 11:32 (NKJV), *"…but the people who know their God shall be strong, and carry out great exploits."*

## SURVIVAL MODE

Consider Nehemiah and the most famous task he completed—rebuilding the wall of Jerusalem. The wall had been down for 142 years. During that time the people were under constant threat of annihilation from the surrounding nations. For 142 years they were in survival mode. Survival mode keeps you focused on the immediate and the short term. People in survival mode have no room in their thinking processes for developing long-range strategic plans. The life of God's people for several generations was day-to-day survival. They could not comprehend building a wall of protection around their city because they were too worried about their sons and daughters being captured during the night and sold into slavery.

Knowing all this, and knowing that he could not build the wall himself, Nehemiah left Susa fully supplied with lumber and finances to complete the task. He also knew he would most likely engage these same hostile neighbors because he represented a threat to the status quo. It is my belief that Nehemiah knew the wall was going to be built when he began praying for God's favor with the king.

## PEOPLE WHO UNDERSTAND AUTHORITY

Nehemiah was a strategic thinker who saw the big picture. He understood that God's provision for him, for the assignment, and for his people would come through the designated lines of authority in his life. The king whom

Nehemiah faithfully served as a Jew in exile was in fact God's instrument of provision, protection, and authority. I have always found it interesting that Nehemiah, with his passion for the task that God had given him, understood the importance of being "designated" by his earthly king for the task.

While the king of Persia was God's instrument of provision for his trip, Nehemiah correctly acknowledged that the hand of God was the deciding factor. In Nehemiah 2:7-8 he says:

> *And I said to the king, "If it please the king, let letters be given me for the governors of the provinces beyond the River, that they may allow me to pass through until I come to Judah, and a letter to Asaph the keeper of the king's forest, that he may give me timber to make beams for the gates of the fortress which is by the temple, for the wall of the city and for the house to which I will go." And the king granted them to me because the good hand of my God was on me.*

Leaders like Nehemiah are people with a clear understanding of authority. Because of his long-standing, faithful relationship to the king of Persia, Nehemiah's project was fully funded by his employer. If Nehemiah had been constantly complaining to the king about his working conditions; if he had been constantly complaining about not making enough money; if he had criticized the king's leadership to subordinates—somehow I don't believe God could have used this relationship He had established for the benefit of a nation to finance the building of the wall. I don't believe Nehemiah would have met God's qualifications to lead this effort to rebuild the walls.

## WE CANNOT OPERATE IN SEDITION AND REBELLION

Nehemiah did not operate in rebellion, and if we are to solve the problems of today's world with God's solutions, neither can we. These leaders must be faithful people in their churches, though they may not sit on elder boards or be "visible." They may be leaders and influencers for righteousness in their cities or nations yet be people who operate out of the public eye. These people serve as God's catalysts for change, but never through seditious means. They are the ones who articulate the Lord's strategies with the anointing of leadership to mobilize others. It is a question of understanding authority.

King David gave us another example of submission to God's designated authority. Saul and his army were searching for David to kill him. Saul fell asleep in a cave where David and his men were hiding. Even though he was unjustly being pursued by King Saul as his enemy, David resisted the desires of his men and refused to kill Saul while he slept. He honored the man who was currently king, although David had been anointed as the rightful king of Israel. This same level of character is part of the Nehemiah leader.

Once again, it is good for us to be reminded that the Lord's greatest love is people. Nehemiah represented God's desires for people. He expressed God's compassion; he had the Father's heart for the people. These leaders are God's gift to His people. We don't motivate these men and women; we identify them so as to properly align ourselves with them in the days ahead. In times of crisis the Lord will always appoint these anointed men and women to lead.

Nehemiah accepted the assignment God set before him. He was inspired and anointed by Him to fulfill the assignment, and the necessary resources followed his leadership. God caused all of these things to happen to Nehemiah and every other leader like him in Scripture, and He will cause them to happen to us today. The circumstances today may be different, but the principles are timeless and relevant. This is God's way. Step into what He has for you.

## E N D N O T E

1. *The Works of Josephus, Volume III, Antiquities of the Jews, Book XI* (Grand Rapids, MI: Baker Book House, 1974), 120.

# CHAPTER 7

## *Questions for Consideration*

1. We live in perilous times. What do you think will bring about God's solutions to the seemingly unsolvable problems we are facing?

_____

_____

_____

_____

_____

2. Are you aware of an assignment God has given you that seems impossible?

_____

_____

_____

3. Are you positioning yourself to fulfill that assignment?

_____

_____

_____

_____

_____

_____

_____

_____

_____

4. Are you willing to use the skills God has placed in your heart to fulfill this assignment?

_____

_____

_____

_____

_____

_____

_____

_____

_____

5. Are you willing to risk everything to do it? What are you not willing to risk?

_____

_____

_____

_____

_____

_____

_____

_____

_____

_____

# CHAPTER 8

## Anointed Leadership Will Face Opposition

*Now it came about that when Sanballat heard that we were rebuilding the wall, he became furious and very angry and mocked the Jews. He spoke in the presence of his brothers and the wealthy men of Samaria and said, "What are these feeble Jews doing? Are they going to restore it for themselves? Can they offer sacrifices? Can they finish in a day? Can they revive the stones from the dusty rubble even the burned ones?" Now Tobiah the Ammonite was near him and he said, "Even what they are building—if a fox should jump on it, he would break their stone wall down!" Hear, O our God, how we are despised! Return their reproach on their own heads and give them up for plunder in a land of captivity* (Nehemiah 4:1-4).

When God assigns a work of change or restoration to one of His leaders, opposition always comes. The enemy of our soul tries to oppose everything God initiates. He will try to oppose evangelistic crusades, but he will also try to oppose business deals dedicated to generating millions for the Kingdom.

He tries to oppose unity among pastors, but he will also try to oppose a government leader who uses his position and influence to end corruption in his nation. The enemy is committed to isolating our religious leaders to bring about their moral failure, but he is just as committed to the moral failure of a CEO who has dedicated profits from his business to the Kingdom. Our pastors need intercessors and prayer so they can stand against the schemes of the enemy, but so does the godly educator who is given the task of molding the hearts and minds of the next generation. It is critically important to understand that the enemy will try to oppose every strategy of God, whether it is a strategy for a church, a business, a government, a hospital, or a school.

## BIG ASSIGNMENT, BIG OPPOSITION

All leaders will experience opposition in some fashion. Leaders who execute the strategies of God face opposition on a different level. The bigger the assignment is, the greater the opposition appears to be.

In Nehemiah 4:1-4, Sanballat, the governor of Samaria, and Tobiah were in positions of influence over the remnant in Israel. We have seen that the Jews were without a walled city for protection. According to Nehemiah chapter 1, their existence was miserable. To their oppressors, they also represented a tax base and a source of income. They were enslaved or sold into slavery. They were oppressed by their conquerors, heavily taxed, and living a difficult existence. Sanballat, one of the king of Persia's governors, was undoubtedly one of their chief oppressors and a source of great misery.

Nehemiah's arrival in Jerusalem as the governor of Judah came with the king's authorization. Nehemiah therefore represented an unwanted challenge to the members of the ruling elite, who despised and dominated the Jews in every way. The Temple had been built many years before by Joshua, the priest, and Zerubbabel, the governor.

Regular temple services were tolerated by Sanballat because they posed no real threat to him. However, the construction of a wall of protection around Jerusalem represented a threat of an entirely different nature. Sanballat and his leaders reacted to someone seeking the welfare of a people who represented their economic base. The wall of Jerusalem would also change the economics of the region for Sanballat.

## UNDERSTANDING OPPOSITION

In our day, we will see a new generation of leaders being positioned in government, business, education, media, finance, and ministry to be catalysts for change. Understanding and overcoming opposition is part of leadership and part of this change. These verses in Nehemiah 4 provide us with an illustration of the nature of opposition and the appropriate responses to this opposition.

The people in positions of influence and power, who had a vested interest in the status quo, opposed the change this wall would bring. They had exercised a physical and economic domination over the poor of the land. Jesus said:

> *…You know that the rulers of the Gentiles lord it over them, and their great men exercise authority over them. It is not this way among you…* (Matthew 20:25-26).

Leadership that dominates, controls, or manipulates others, whether it is in a family, in a business, or in government, has no place in the Kingdom Economy. Jesus is our model for leadership. Nowhere do we see the Son of God dominating, manipulating, or exercising a controlling nature over others. It is important to make this clear distinction here.

## GOD MEASURES PERSONAL ASSETS DIFFERENTLY

For Nehemiah and the builders of the wall, part of the outside opposition came in the form of mockery and ridicule. The text says these leaders laughed among themselves and mocked the "feeble Jews." Their mockery implied God's people could not bring about change because they were inferior and powerless. The mockers must have thought, *The walls have been broken down for 142 years. Surely these Jews don't really think they can change things?* Yet while Sanballat, Tobiah, and their friends were meeting to collectively disparage God's people, the Jews under Nehemiah's leadership were laying one stone upon another.

When God plans for the welfare of people, opposition is assured. The face of His strategy is the leader God chooses to represent Him. Leaders are opposed by those who are threatened by the change God wants to bring to a people, a ministry, a business, a city, or a nation. They may be ridiculed as inferior and as not capable of effecting this change. They may be accused of being powerless and lacking the proper influence and resources. All of these things may, in fact, be true. Yet, the apostle Paul said it best, *"…for when I am weak, then I am strong"* (2 Cor. 12:10).

## Resumé Limitations Don't Hinder God

God is not limited by an unimpressive resumé or lack of management experience. Our inabilities can actually be our assets in the Kingdom of God. This in no way minimizes the importance of experience. Authority in life is gained through experience and there is no substitute for that. However, God is not limited by our lack of experience to bring about this change.

Though Nehemiah had served an important role in the king's court, it is likely he had never been to a school of leadership. Though he was a faithful and trusted servant of the king, he probably had no massive construction projects on his resumé. Yet God was not limited by Nehemiah's lack of experience—and we are still talking about this feat 2,500 years later. He had natural gifts and talents, but his real strength was his weakness in these areas. He saw God's vision for the people, accepted the assignment, and was given grace to communicate the vision. Then God enabled the wall builders to "see" the vision. This anointing for a special kind of leadership produced the change.

## FAITHFULNESS DURING OBSCURITY BRINGS PROMOTION

Real change comes by God working through men and women who understand they are doomed to failure without Him. Our personal assortments of strengths and abilities are not necessarily what bring success. It is the surrender of those strengths and abilities to the throne of God that makes them like a scalpel in the hands of a skilled surgeon. God wants to utilize the skill sets He has given us. However, their highest and best use comes out of their surrender.

We find the success God wants because we position ourselves for only one option—victory. In the Kingdom Economy, what may look like defeat to others can be the seeds of success. When leaders accept God's assignment to lead, the authority, resources, and influence of Heaven are at their disposal. This becomes delegation of real authority to represent God's strategies to bring on significant cultural change.

The process of that delegation does not happen if we have not established a history of faithfulness in times of obscurity. In the Kingdom, big jobs require humble leadership, which is being faithful to the King. It is apparent that Nehemiah had established this history of faithfulness in times of obscurity before the assignment and the requisite authority.

Nehemiah took Sanballat's and Tobiah's threats seriously and did what all good leaders must do: *"But we prayed to our God, and because of them we set up a guard against them day and night"* (Neh. 4:9). The building of the wall posed a threat to the economics of the region. When your plans pose a threat to the opposition's economics, you also threaten the spirit of mammon (greed). Sometimes the core of this kind of opposition is what the Bible refers to as "the love of money" (see Heb. 13:5; 1 Tim. 6:10). Nehemiah prayed, but he also set up a guard. The prayer was for God's protection and the guard was set to defend to the death His purpose for Jerusalem and the people.

## Opposition From Within

*"So it was, when the Jews who dwelt near them came, that they told us ten times, 'From whatever place you turn, they will be upon us'"* (Neh. 4:12 NKJV). Nehemiah also faced opposition from fearful and timid allies. In many ways, this was more difficult to address because it was more subtle and less defined.

Some Jews did not participate in the labor of building the wall. They lived in the surrounding areas and were timid observers of what was taking place. They watched their friends and neighbors leave their fields and families to labor day and night on this wall under the threat of death and failure. They may have hoped for their neighbors' success, but the price of participation was just too high for them to pay.

These fearful "allies" may have said, "This wall has been down for 142 years. Yes, it is uncomfortable, and we are oppressed by the neighboring nations, but it is better to live in bondage than to die for a wall. Who is this Nehemiah anyway?"

These neighbors would bring intelligence to the workers about the devilish plans of Sanballat and Tobiah. However, along with the intelligence they brought their fear and timidity even though they would benefit from the labor of their friends. The timid many times want to impose their fear on those who would risk everything for the goal.

Their messages of fear and discouragement spread quickly among the people. However, Nehemiah was not only God's man to lead the construction project, but he also represented much more. Godly leadership can make no provision for fear in the process of change. Nehemiah challenged the leaders and the people to do three things: keep working, remember their God, and fight.

## HOW MUST LEADERS LEAD?

- **By Having a Clear Vision**—Transformational type change in a business, government, or ministry requires leadership. The leader must have a clear vision. He or she must be able to see the destination in order to articulate the journey to those who will follow. If you don't have this vision for your life, pray and seek God for it. Ask Him to give you His vision for your life. Ask Him to give you this vision for change and keep asking until it comes. The clear vision will sustain you. God permits a clear vision for change to enable His leaders to have a supernatural resolve when challenges come.

- **By Seeing the Finished Work**—I believe that Nehemiah saw the wall as a finished work after his three months of prayer and fasting in Susa. He must have told the Lord he would take this seemingly impossible job as his own. To Nehemiah it was not a question of if the wall would be built, but how quickly. God allows His leaders to see the finished work before it has begun. This happened with Moses and many other great men and women of Scripture.

- **By Praying and Setting a Guard**—I have always been impressed by the supernatural resolve displayed by Nehemiah. This resolve was necessary when he encountered opposition from those who were threatened by God's plan for the welfare of His people. The opposition was serious, direct, and life threatening. Nehemiah's response was to pray and ask for the Lord's protection and to set a guard. Faith requires that we meet God's grace and protecting hand with individual and collective effort. Pray and "set a guard."

- **By Reminding People of Their Purpose, Their God, and Their Strength to Fight**—When God implants us with His vision, as with Nehemiah, opposition will come from timid and fearful allies who don't believe the task can or should be done. At that point, the louder voice must come from Romans 8:14-15: *"For all who are being led by the Spirit of God, these are sons of God. For you have not received a spirit of slavery leading to fear again, but you have received a spirit of adoption as sons by which we cry out, 'Abba! Father!'"* The Spirit of God is the One who influences our actions, not timid or fearful allies, or condescending colleagues. Timid and fearful allies will try to impose their fear on others. Fear has its greatest impact when people feel powerless and helpless. Leadership reminds people of their purpose, their God, and their strength to fight.

## THE ASSIGNMENT BRINGS THE OPPOSITION

In speaking of the last days, Jesus spoke of a time when insurmountable problems would cause people's hearts to fail them. Those who are called to implement God's strategies in our day will be special leaders. Clearly, this is a higher level of leadership. These are leaders in the mold of Nehemiah who are inspired by the Lord and anointed and equipped by Him to perform their tasks with supernatural resolve, dedication, and insight. When God gives an assignment, it is the assignment that brings the opposition. However, the face of the assignment is His leader. The apostle Paul said it best:

> *For our struggle is not against flesh and blood, but against the rulers, against the powers, against the world forces of this darkness...* (Ephesians 6:12).

We must identify these leaders and support them in their work of transformation because they are God's gift to our nations.

# CHAPTER 8

## *Questions for Consideration*

1. Have you ever felt like the Lord may have been speaking to you about a particular task or assignment, but you didn't obey because it didn't seem convenient?

_____

_____

_____

_____

_____

_____

_____

_____

_____

_____

2. Has the Lord spoken to you about a calling of leadership on your life, either by giving you a knowing or by speaking to you through His Word?

_____

_____

_____

_____

_____

_____

_____

_____


3. Do you feel the Lord has directed you to your city, nation, or region? If this is the case, you have an assignment. Have you sought the Lord for that assignment?

_____

_____

_____

_____

_____

_____

_____

_____

_____

# CHAPTER 9

## *God Gives the Power to Get Wealth*

*Then you say in your heart, "My power and the might of my hand have gained me this wealth." And you shall remember the LORD your God, for it is He who gives you power to get wealth, that He may establish His covenant which He swore to your fathers, as it is this day* (Deuteronomy 8:17-18 NKJV).

In this chapter of Deuteronomy, Moses is giving the nation of Israel one of his final exhortations. He begins by telling them they are to remember what God did for them during their 40 years of wilderness struggle. He recounts God's faithfulness and testing through the manna. He tells them in Deuteronomy 8:3, *"…that man does not live by bread alone, but man lives by every word that proceeds out of the mouth of the LORD."* Moses reminds them about God's parental chastening. Describing their 40 years of struggle he says, *"Your clothing did not wear out on you, nor did your foot swell…"* (Deut. 8:4). He tells them God was with them during all their struggles.

He also speaks of a future time and place where they will eat good food, their crops will flourish, they will live in houses they didn't build, and their land will receive a supernatural blessing of productivity. I'm sure while Moses was communicating this to God's people, they were jumping up and down in anticipation of this future time. After all, they had lived for generations in the bondage of Egypt with lack and deprivation.

They walked for 40 years in the desert, wandering "aimlessly" because of the promise of a new land that had not yet materialized. They had "endured" God's daily provision of the manna. Yes, God had personally given manna. Yes, He told Moses it was for the purpose of testing them to see if they would obey His commandments. But the same diet for 40 years?! They must have been excited about the new day that was coming.

## "You Will Lack Nothing"

In the first ten verses of Deuteronomy 8, Moses is telling the people they *"will not lack anything"* for God Himself was *"bringing* [them] *into a good land."* God's hand would be upon everything. Moses is saying, *"…your herds and your flocks* [will] *multiply"; "your silver and gold* [will] *multiply";* and *"all that you have* [will] *multiply"* (see Deut. 8:13).

The good thing about all this is that God was going to make it happen! They probably thought, *He must have seen our struggle and decided to reward us.* Remember, Moses was speaking to men and women who would become small business owners, farmers, and shepherds. He was speaking a language that every business owner, farmer, or employee gets excited about—prosperity!

# We Jump Out of Our Seats!

In a discourse like this, this is usually the place where we, as God's representatives in the marketplace, are jumping out of our seats with anticipation of what is to come. To people like us, this message of Moses translates something like this: "God is going to help me make a lot of money"; "increased cash flow for my business"; "higher profits"; "I'm going to get a big promotion"; "a new car"; "a bigger house"; "it's going to get easier"; "my destination is in sight"; "I'm going to the United States!"

Over the years, the inner man hasn't changed that much. I'm relatively certain Moses' audience of a few million people were daydreaming about all these wonderful things they were going to "get." Their desires and dreams were about to come to pass in the near future. Moses had everyone's attention by this point. Then he concludes the promise of a new prosperity on land they hadn't tilled, houses they hadn't built, and a special rain that was coming to their fields directly from God. He says the following under the inspiration of the Holy Spirit, *"Beware that you do not forget the Lord your God…"* (Deut. 8:11).

# Success Can Insulate Us

Success, and the pride that sometimes accompanies it, will insulate us from the humility that is necessary to approach the Lord and receive His tangible benefits. We see and hear people in the marketplace say with their lips or their actions what Deuteronomy 8:17 says, *"…My power and the strength of my hand made me this wealth."*

Sometimes we view this kind of prosperity as the goal or destination for our lives. We see personal genius or effort as the reason for individual blessing and give begrudging acknowledgment to the Lord. We consider our wisdom and judgment in the deal indispensable. God may have sprinkled a little dust from Heaven on the deal, but He played a secondary role, at best. The deal becomes a reward we are due, and one that carries very little responsibility with it, other than perhaps a tithe as a tip for God's participation, however small it might have been.

In this scenario, we always come back to the fundamental question: ownership. Who really makes it happen and who owns the blessing? Sometimes we get a little possessive with what really belongs to the Lord. We discussed the issue of ownership in a previous chapter. But the overriding question here is: Where then does the ability to prosper really come from?

## He Gives Us the Power

Moses answered that question in Deuteronomy 8:18:

*And you shall remember the Lord your God, for it is He who gives you power to get wealth, that He may establish His covenant which He swore to your fathers, as it is this day* (NKJV).

The Hebrew word for *wealth* in this verse means "power, riches, substance, a force of men, means or other resources or goods."[1] Everything we have or will ever get, everything we will ever accomplish, is because of the Lord's grace in our lives. Even the capacity to make money is because of God giving His people this ability. Deuteronomy 8:18 is clear: it is God who causes this to happen. Clearly it is within God's ability to do this for His people. He controls much more than we realize!

The Kingdom Economy will soon be the dominant economic system on the earth. Even now, the Lord is preparing His representatives in the marketplace for this coming time. In the days ahead, those who will succeed in this economy will be His servants who understand this principle. The Lord gives us His prophetic insight, ability, sound judgment, wisdom, and the understanding of complex financial issues to generate this kind of income. It is because of Him, not our own personal genius (see Exod. 31:6).

Over and over again the Scripture says that God puts skill, wisdom, or a unique discernment for a particular occupation in us. Even the personal genius we may have for a particular business is ours only because He has given it to us. He always gives it with a purpose: "to establish His covenant" (see Deut. 8:18). The reason for wealth and the power to get it is the establishment of His Kingdom. When we understand and walk in Deuteronomy 8:18, we will literally shake the world.

## CONTAINER OR CONDUIT OF HIS BLESSINGS

God does want us to enjoy the benefits, but He has a broader purpose than us and our personal comfort. He wants His people to be conduits of His blessings for the purpose of the Kingdom, not containers of the blessing.

Why is this understanding important to people in the marketplace? *Truth always produces liberty in the Kingdom of God.* I have met marketplace people all over the world who have been deeply impacted by these few verses in Deuteronomy. They have been liberated by the knowledge that it is the Lord who "gives us the power to get wealth." We don't have to depend on our limited knowledge to always make the right decisions.

He is the One who makes available His unlimited knowledge of all factors necessary to get wealth. He does not need to study economic trends to predict what will happen in the economy next year—He already knows what is going to happen. This information is made available to every investor who first acknowledges that God has the information, and second, seeks Him for it. The pressure is not on you to produce but on the Lord to make it happen.

## A NEW BREED IS EMERGING

Now that we have established this foundation, we will look at another group of men and women in the marketplace. Skilled professional men and women all over the world are setting up profit-making businesses for the sole purpose of generating great amounts of money for the harvest of souls worldwide. These men and women are seasoned marketplace people who are gifted in business. They will be satisfied and fulfilled with nothing less than funding the cultural transformation of entire cities and nations.

These men and women don't think about supporting one missionary; they think about an army of missionaries. They don't think about one church; they think about filling an entire nation with churches. They don't think about sending money for a daily food allowance to one young orphan in Africa; they dream about building a network of orphanages throughout the continent to get every orphan off the streets.

This is not just their dream; it is God's desire! As marketplace leaders we need to think bigger, wider thoughts and find ways to utilize our contacts and our gifts to make the will of God come into the earth.

## Kingdom Alliances

All over the world men and women are coming together to form Kingdom alliances. These alliances are anointed teams who use profit-making ventures to generate funds for the harvest of souls and ministry to the poor. God will give these men and women creative, profit-making ideas while they sleep. They have a special anointing for leadership in business or government. You may not find them in the pulpits of churches. They may not be elders in the church. Most of them prefer to conduct their work in private, away from the spotlight of man, yet under the spotlight of Heaven.

They wake in the middle of the night to pray for the Kingdom to come. Their night-time prayer is recorded in Psalm 2:8: *"Ask of Me, and I will surely give the nations as Your inheritance, and the very ends of the earth as Your possession."* Their profit-making enterprises will play a dominant role in the implementation of last-days strategies in the days ahead. These men and women understand the sanctity of the role they have been given.

## A Holy Calling

Some religious leaders understand that these men and women are called to a holy calling. They have been commissioned to this work by the Holy Spirit. They are leaders who burn with a fire of God to generate millions for the Kingdom. They may not testify in front of people about their work, but they sit faithfully in churches week after week. They have already been commissioned by the Holy Spirit. Their commissioning may be in private times of prayer. They may never pastor a church, yet their calling is just as holy and they walk humbly before the Lord. They live Deuteronomy 8:18!

Pastors must learn how to pastor these men and women. They are young entrepreneurs, wealthy corporate executives, retired people of influence, physicians, lawyers, educators, government leaders, skilled workers, or homemakers, but they are all people of prayer with a mission. They are not called to a "higher calling" or a "lower calling" but to the holy calling of making money for the end-time harvest.

ENDNOTE

1. James Strong, S.T.D., LL.D., *A Concise Dictionary of the Words in the Hebrew Bible* (Madison, NJ: Strong, 1890), 39.

# CHAPTER 9

## *Questions for Consideration*

1. Do you get excited about the message of God's prosperity for His people?

_____

_____

_____

_____

_____

_____

_____

_____

_____

_____

2. Do you get equally excited about the responsibility that comes with God's prosperity?

_____

_____

_____

_____

_____

_____

_____

_____

_____

3. Have you ever considered your business savvy, your intelligence, or your personality as the indispensable commodity to a profit-making venture?

_____

_____

_____

_____

_____

_____

_____

_____

_____

4. In Deuteronomy 8:18, we find a verse that should be memorized by every believer in the business world. Why do you think God includes the word "remember"?

_____

_____

_____

_____

_____

_____

_____

_____

_____

# CHAPTER 10

## *Favor Is God's Instrument of Change*

*The LORD was with Joseph, and he was a successful man; and he was in the house of his master the Egyptian. And his master saw that the LORD was with him and that the LORD made all he did to prosper in his hand. So Joseph found favor in his sight, and served him. Then he made him overseer of his house, and all that he had he put under his authority* (Genesis 39:2-4 NKJV).

Before business meetings, we pray for favor. When we argue a court case, we ask God for it. Salespeople around the world seek for the favor of God over their prospects. People in the marketplace around the world pray for favor in business ventures, investments, businesses, governments, elections, families, and relationships. I have discovered that many pastors know more about the favor of God than we do. They seem to live expecting it and oftentimes they recognize God's favor on their congregants.

Most of us in the marketplace hope for the favor of God, and leaders in every nation desire it as a sign of God's validation of their efforts. Favor is one of the most sought after, prayed for, spoken about, and cherished gifts from God, yet one of the least understood. We find it difficult to define and don't know how to react when we get it. Just what is this thing called "favor"?

## A Measure of Favor to Us All

The Bible is filled with references to the favor of God. Ruth received it from Boaz; King David lived a life of worship, gratitude, and favor; and Saul misused God's favor and eventually rejected it by his disobedience and disdain for God's ways. Samuel and Jesus grew in it before God and man. Mary had the envied position before the Lord as "highly favored" (see Luke 1:28 NKJV). Joseph had favor even when he was in prison and didn't recognize it.

The Jews left Egypt with the wealth of Egyptians because of the favor of God. From the time of Abraham until today, God's people have sought for, walked in, and experienced the favor of God as a transforming influence on their lives.

When our lives are brought into proper alignment with God the Father, a measure of His favor is there for us all. The favor comes to us because of this relationship. It is our due, so to speak. The Hebrew word for *favor* means "to encompass or surround; delight; pleasure...."[1] The favor of God can be an expression of His delight and pleasure with us.

While God's favor can be His personal expression to us as individuals, we tend to lose sight of the fact that it is also strategic in nature.

## No Outward Qualifications

Joseph spent years in prison after he was falsely accused of rape. When Potiphar's wife desired Joseph, he honored God at a moment of potential compromise by fleeing. Yet he was unjustly imprisoned. Joseph had the opportunity to become hardened by his surroundings and bitter toward God and others. Some scholars say Joseph spent 12 years in prison and some say two years. Even if he only spent two years in an Egyptian prison, it was too long!

For many years I ministered to prison inmates. Prison is a place where men, in particular, withdraw from other inmates as a means of protection. It does not matter whether you are incarcerated in Africa, South America, or the United States, the prevailing mindset is still the same: withdraw and keep to yourself for your own protection.

I think it is reasonable to assume that an Egyptian prison thousands of years ago was an unpleasant place. Yet even under difficult circumstances, Joseph displayed a tenderness that must have pleased the Lord. I have always been amazed at the "pastoral concern" Joseph expressed to the two servants of Pharaoh: *"Why do you look so sad today?"* (Gen. 40:7 NKJV). After hearing that the two men had dreams they could not interpret, he acknowledged the Lord as the source of his gift of interpretation by saying, *"Do not interpretations belong to the Lord?"* (Gen. 40:8 NKJV).

We all know how Joseph stood before Pharaoh and was given a role in the history of God's people that is acknowledged thousands of years later by Jew and Gentile. However, his outward qualifications for this kind of leadership were nonexistent and apparently unimportant. His inward qualifications were what caused this kind of favor to come to Joseph. His character, integrity, and faithfulness positioned him for the level of favor needed to implement God's strategic purpose for a nation of people yet to come.

## God's Instrument for Change

God's favor will produce radical results through people who have "earned" this kind of favor by lives of holiness, integrity, faithfulness, and commitment—when no one is watching. When Joseph ran from Potiphar's wife, only two people were in that room. Yet thousands of years later, the entire world knows about a righteous decision that young man made. His decision was not so private after all. Joseph proved to be a man who could be trusted with the higher level of favor that was needed to fulfill the assignment of preparing the way for a nation.

King David said it best in Psalm 101:2-3 (NIV):

*I will be careful to lead a blameless life—when will You come to me? I will walk in my house with blameless heart. I will set before my eyes no vile thing. The deeds of faithless men I hate; they will not cling to me.*

In a word, we must be people God can trust with unusual authority, finances, public positions, or influence. Then He can trust us to carry out His plan with humility and honor because we have proved ourselves faithful during the difficult times.

## Look at the Big Picture

Joseph's greatest challenge was not the prison but later, when unusual favor put him in a position of enormous influence, power, and wealth. His brothers stood before him, fearful and surprised at the sight of the brother they had hated and sold for a few pieces of silver. This was Joseph's greatest challenge. He responded with strategic understanding beyond his personal pain. Genesis 45:5 says, *"…do not therefore be grieved or angry with yourselves because you sold me here; for God sent me before you to preserve life"* (NKJV). Joseph was a man who understood the big picture. This is so very difficult to do sometimes. But we must learn to look for the strategic nature of what we perceive as a prison. We must ask God to show us the big picture.

## The Danger

We face a danger when the favor of God comes to us. We need to recognize that this favor always comes for a purpose beyond us. *Favor is usually coupled with an assignment. The favor is how the assignment gets accomplished.* The favor comes from God, and when we misrepresent the situation, exaggerate our importance, or fail to acknowledge the Lord's hand, we jeopardize our opportunity for another assignment.

The Lord is doing unusual things with ordinary people who live and work every day in the marketplace. It is critical that we carry the responsibility that comes with the assignment with humility. When we step into the assignment and operate in the favor that comes with it, we have a tendency to exaggerate our role or our importance to the outcome.

Favor is simply a gift to us from an all-powerful God with a strategic plan for the world. When we live our lives daily in this kind of favor, we represent the Giver with humility and honor. We must resist the temptation to violate the principle outlined in Proverbs 3:6-7:

> *In all your ways acknowledge Him, and He shall direct your paths. Do not be wise in your own eyes; fear the Lord and depart from evil* (NKJV).

## Different Levels

*Unmerited* is a word frequently used to describe the favor of God. In one sense, this kind of favor is unmerited because we don't deserve the blessings God gives. But there is another kind of favor that is "earned." Joseph earned the favor he received to lead Egypt when he ran from Potiphar's wife. In Potiphar's house he still had the favor of God, but to lead Egypt God had to give him a different level of favor. In order to be ready for the second level, he had to be tested while he was walking in the first level. Psalm 105:17-19 says:

> *He sent a man before them, Joseph, who was sold as a slave. They afflicted his feet with fetters, he himself was*

*laid in irons; until the time that His word came to pass, the word of the LORD tested him.*

God is the ultimate multitasker and He does it every time to perfection! God was testing Joseph to see if he would be able to handle the second level of favor. He was setting conditions in Egypt for Joseph's promotion while He was keeping His covenant with Abraham and preparing a place for a small family that would become a nation of people.

At the same time that we may be experiencing difficulties or even receiving God's favor on lower levels than we expect, God may be working in our lives to cause us to succeed on higher levels.

## BIG ASSIGNMENTS REQUIRE HUMILITY

I have a friend who was a high-level government leader in his nation. Many years ago, when I first met him in Washington DC, the Lord clearly spoke to me, "I will make this man president of his nation." I was shocked by this, and for several years I told no one but just prayed for him. This man has no political ambitions. He is, however, totally committed to God's plan for his life and his nation.

Recently I said to him, "Brother, you know your greatest challenge will be after the Lord sets you in place as president. The challenge for you will be not to believe what people say about you. You will need honest people around you."

His response astounded me. "Paul, the moment I believe what people say about me or take credit for anything the Lord does through me, His blessing on my nation will flow through my fingers like dry sand."

This is a man who walks in the highest kind of favor and has earned the trust of the Lord. Leaders must learn about God's favor and the responsibility to carry it as His ambassadors. Big assignments require high levels of favor. Higher levels are given to humble leaders.

## HOW DO WE RECEIVE THIS FAVOR?

Favor is also a way we find the direction of the Lord. Many times we don't have this favor because we don't ask for it. It is appropriate that we ask Him daily for His favor. We can live in expectation of a life of favor, but it is appropriate for us to ask Him. For years I have prayed to the Lord, "Today, Lord, let me see Your favor, that I may follow it." I have learned that God's favor is many times a direction for our lives. Ask Him for His favor over your families, your children, your relationships, your future, your meetings, your ventures—ask Him for His favor on everything you touch. When He gives it, acknowledge Him as the giver, not only in private but in public.

Everything God does has a purpose beyond personal blessing. A profitable business venture probably has a greater purpose than just padding your net worth. Find out what God's purpose is and commit to it without reservation. The favor of God is given to bring His Kingdom to the world. Ask Him to make you a chalice worthy of the kind of favor that will produce change in businesses, governments, and nations.

# Favor Brings Measurable Results

I used to think that favor was a fuzzy, ethereal, spiritual concept by which we gained some personal fulfillment. The more I studied, the more I began to realize that God's favor always produces tangible results. His favor is concrete, yet mystical at the same time. It is a gift God dispenses to His people—all of His people.

God's favor will produce solid and tangible results in our families, our businesses, our governments, and our lives. We can ask Him for it when we are about to enter difficult meetings, make sales calls, plead a case before a judge, or run for election. We must learn to recognize it, both on ourselves and on others, and acknowledge the favor of God.

The challenge for many of us is to live expecting His favor every day, all day, and not just hoping for it. When we are living our lives according to His principles, the favor of God is our status in life. It may look different in each case, but this is how we are to live in the Kingdom. Favor is a spiritual force that changes events, people, and communities. It is a force that God uses with leaders.

# Righteousness: The Standard of the Kingdom Economy

In order to live life in God's favor and walk in the higher levels of His favor, we must walk before the Lord with integrity in all areas of our lives. I have learned I can leave no stone unturned. We must be ruthless when the enemy sets before us the temptation to sin. We are to give no place for evil in our dealings with people, either in our actions or our thoughts. Righteousness is the standard of the Kingdom Economy. Righteousness is the standard not only in our personal lives, but also in our business dealings with others.

In the Kingdom Economy, secrets don't stay secrets long. Remember Joseph and Potiphar's wife and the solitude of that room? Yet the whole world knows of Joseph's decision today.

## Summary Points

In summary, here are some things about this powerful instrument that are worth considering:

- God's favor has the capacity to move you from obscurity to a position of influence.

- Favor is a powerful instrument that the Lord uses to produce change in your life. God's favor was what brought about the change in Joseph's life, and it is His favor that brings about change and promotion in your life.

- Favor comes with an assignment. God's favor is how the assignment gets accomplished. Bigger assignments require a higher level of His favor. The higher level of His favor can only be placed in a vessel that has been tested and proved a worthy vessel to contain it.

- Favor will produce concrete, tangible results in your life, your business, your family, and over your government and nation. It is tangible and mystical at the same time. Ask God for it.

- The favor of God is extended to the righteous by a sovereign God. He controls how much He gives, to whom, and when He gives it. The one who receives the gift has no control over the gift, other than to ask for it from the Giver.

- Many times, others will see the results of God's favor on your life before you do. It is not unusual to not recognize His favor.

- There are two types of God's favor—favor with God and favor with man. Many times the favor of God on a person will produce favor with man. (see 1 Sam. 2:26).

- Favor is an essential ingredient in the life of every believer, no matter what nation you are from or what position you have in life. Favor is a gift God gives to His people without regard for status, income, or education. It doesn't matter whether you are the owner of a small restaurant in Nicaragua or the CEO of a multi-national corporation in London—His favor is available to you. It is bigger than your personal success, comfort, or promotion. God always has the bigger purpose in mind. In Joseph's case, favor was given to him, not just for his personal promotion but for the sake of a small group of people (Jacob's family) who would soon become the nation of Israel.

- God gives this deeper level of favor to those who have positioned themselves for it by making right choices, by allowing the Lord to break and mold them, by conducting their lives with integrity and honor before Him, and by acknowledging Him in all their ways. This deeper operation of favor will come upon men and women in the marketplace to lead or bring about change in governments, businesses, educational systems, or organizations. God's purpose is to bring about cultural transformation through the Kingdom of God. His favor paves the way.

## ENDNOTE

1. James Strong, S.T.D., LL.D., *A Concise Dictionary of the Words in the Hebrew Bible* (Madison, NJ: Strong, 1890), 39.

# CHAPTER 10

## *Questions for Consideration*

1. When you prayed for God's favor and it came, have you ever asked God to show you His purpose beyond your personal blessing?

_____

_____

_____

_____

_____

2. Have there been times in your own life when God's favor also produced a favor with those in authority over you?

_____

_____

_____

_____

_____

_____

3. When God gives us His favor for big assignments, this favor brings with it big responsibilities to honor Him. Have you fulfilled those obligations when these assignments came in the past?

_____

_____

_____

_____

_____

_____

_____

4. Have you ever considered that God's favor produces tangible results in your life? Describe some ways His favor has done this for you.

_____

_____

_____

_____

_____

_____

5. Have you ever noticed God's favor in the lives of other leaders?

_____

_____

_____

_____

_____

_____

_____

_____

# CHAPTER 11

## *Service Before Leadership— Serving God in Government*

*Thus says the Lord GOD of hosts, "Come, go to this steward, to Shebna, who is in charge of the royal household, 'What right do you have here, and whom do you have here, that you have hewn a tomb for yourself here, you who hew a tomb on the height, you who carve a resting place for yourself in the rock? 'Behold, the LORD is about to hurl you headlong, O man. And He is about to grasp you firmly and roll you tightly like a ball, to be cast into a vast country; there you will die and there your splendid chariots will be, you shame of your master's house.' I will depose you from your office, and I will pull you down from your station. Then it will come about in that day, that I will summon My servant Eliakim the son of Hilkiah, and I will clothe him with your tunic and tie your sash securely about him. I will entrust him with your authority, and he will become a father to the inhabitants of Jerusalem and to the house of Judah. Then I will set the key of the house of David on his shoulder, when he opens no one will shut, when he shuts no one will open* (Isaiah 22:15-22).

In this text, the Lord speaks through the prophet Isaiah about the destiny of two men in government. One man, Shebna, was a counselor and prime minister/treasurer to Hezekiah, king of Judah. The other, Eliakim, was an obscure leader from an insignificant family with little influence.

Shebna was corrupt, arrogant, full of pride and selfish ambition, and a man of intrigue who was apparently intoxicated by his position and influence. He did not fear God or respect people he was to lead. Shebna led a group called the Egyptian Party, which believed that Judah needed political alliances with Egypt to offset potential threats from Assyria.

Since Shebna was the leading counselor to the king, his influence and political viewpoint made his group a force in the politics of Judah. The Egyptian Party had an agenda that was clearly opposed to God's influence over government.[1] They believed trusting the Lord for the protection of the nation was not a prudent course of action. When God said He would be their defense, they thought safety for Judah should come from political alliances with other nations, a clear violation of Scripture.

While Shebna was pressing for an alliance with Egypt and pretending concern for Judah, some scholars say he was also secretly giving information to the king of Assyria about the inner counsel of the king he was supposed to serve. Intrigue and secret government meetings have always been completely open to the eyes and ears of the Lord. God exposed these things to the prophet Isaiah and sent him to Shebna with a message that he would be removed from his position.

Isaiah went on to prophesy that God would give Shebna's position and authority to an obscure man named Eliakim (the Hebrew translation means "God will raise up; God raises").[2] There is a lesson for our government leaders in this chapter. God is involved in the affairs of government, and He exercises His influence more than we realize. In our day, He is "raising up" men and women like Eliakim.

## THE AUTHOR OF GOVERNMENT

The Lord is the author of government, order, and structure. He established government to provide a framework of protection and order so that families and communities can flourish. Government is supposed to benefit the people. Consider our admonition from the apostle Paul in Romans 13:1:

> *Every person is to be in subjection to the governing authorities. For there is no authority except from God, and those which exist are established by God.*

The perversion of government is anarchy, corruption, and domination of people for selfish reasons. Eliakim and Shebna represent the two completely different worldviews or kingdoms, as we discussed in Chapter 1.

These same divergent worldviews exist today. One is the Kingdom of God and the other is the kingdom of darkness. Government leadership that expresses the Kingdom view is in the mold of Eliakim in Isaiah 22.

## SUMMONED

The concept of a call to government is sometimes a foreign concept in the religious world. Yet to serve God in government is no less of a calling than serving Him as a pastor, a missionary, or a businessman. In many nations, the culture of government produces corruption, selfish ambition, oppression of the poor, manipulation of the masses, and hoarding of wealth that belongs to the people of the nation.

In many developing nations, religious leaders discourage believers from going into government because government is perceived as an evil culture. Yet we have numerous important biblical models of government leaders, such as Daniel, Nehemiah, and Zerubbabel, to name a few. We need to encourage the men and women who have been anointed for this segment of the marketplace to fulfill their destinies. In my view, men and women with this calling need to be identified and commissioned to serve in this segment of culture.

Certainly corruption is a major issue around the world that prevents economic development and foreign investment. *However, whatever element of culture that God's people abandon is the element we have no policy influence over.* If we abandon government, we certainly will not have righteous government leaders who will legislate Kingdom policies for the people they serve.

Instead of abdicating our place in government, we need to empower a new generation of believers with the call to government. God has established government and we need to bring His strategies and influence into government.

## A "CALL" TO GOVERNMENT

Most pastors, by a special unction of the Holy Spirit, are able to deliver several messages a week, year after year, and never give the same message twice. God equips them to be able to deliver His messages to His people. With the calling, comes the equipping to do something that is unusual and unnatural. The men and women who are called to government have also been divinely equipped to fulfill this task, not only for their own personal gratification but also to bring the Kingdom of God into the places they have been ordained to serve. We may say that their personal destinies or callings are the micro view, while His Kingdom, and our places in that Kingdom, is the macro view.

It is essential that we come to the understanding that God is the One who equips people to fulfill their particular destinies. To say it another way, we have been equipped by God to fulfill the destiny He has for us and that destiny is within a Kingdom context. Remember what the Lord told Moses in Exodus 31:6, *"…and in the hearts of all who are skillful I have put skill…."*

As our world gets "smaller" and information is more readily available, there seems to be a growing understanding of this "call" to government. Men and women with the call to lead in government have been equipped emotionally, intellectually, and spiritually for service in this area. God has given them the skill sets to flourish in this calling.

## WHERE ARE THE GODLY GOVERNMENT LEADERS?

Around the world today millions of people are crying out to the Lord for righteous government leaders. We see injustice and greed in many nations, and many poor and needy are suffering. How can this be, and when will it end? Many of these people are godly believers who are beseeching the God of Heaven for His intervention.

Yet God has given government leaders with His anointing to nations around the world. First Timothy 2:1-2 (NIV) instructs us to pray, *"...for kings and all those in authority, that we may live peaceful and quiet lives in all godliness and holiness."*

God is interested in leaders who enable their citizens to live peaceful and quiet lives. Not only must we pray for leaders in the mold of Eliakim to emerge, but we must identify who they are and align ourselves to support them in every way possible. By doing so, we align ourselves with God's will for our nations.

## "GOVERNMENT IS NOT LIKE BUSINESS"

These words were spoken by one of the leading political figures in our city. She had been successful in business, but felt that God was directing her to serve in government as an elected official. She became one of the leading political voices in our city for many years. She was a woman who succeeded in both worlds. It was a revelation to me when she said, "Business leaders need to understand that government is not like business. You need to run government on sound business principles, but government functions differently from business." If this is true, then a special equipping is needed to flourish in this setting.

## CHARACTERISTICS OF GOVERNMENT LEADERSHIP

What characteristics differentiate government leadership from others? How can these leaders be elevated to positions of influence? How can we know which government leaders are God's choices for nations? These are valid questions that apply to any nation on earth, and they are questions every believer needs to ask. The Lord has always used people like Eliakim. Once again in our day, He is changing the leadership of nations for the sake of the people He loves so much. He is setting in place men and women with hearts like Eliakim.

## SERVICE BEFORE LEADERSHIP

Isaiah 22 illustrates this kind of change in government leadership but also lists some prerequisites God has for these leaders to qualify in the eyes of God. When the Lord told Isaiah that He was going to bring about change, He introduced His choice, Eliakim, as *"My servant"* (see Isa. 22:20). The Hebrew for the word *servant* means "bondservant."[3]

In biblical days a bondservant was a slave who was given his freedom by his master. Instead of living as a free man, he pierced his ear with a sharp instrument into the doorpost of the master's house, signifying that he made a decision to serve as a slave in his master's house for the rest of his life. This was the bondservant's free will decision.

# THE PARADOX OF KINGDOM LEADERSHIP

You cannot lead in the Kingdom in any capacity until you first learn to serve. This is the paradox of Kingdom leadership. How can we be expected to carry out the plan of God if we have not learned to serve Him and follow His instruction? It is apparent that Eliakim had to qualify for the designation of "My servant" during his years of obscurity. Back when Eliakim had no authority, he must have become a man God could trust with the kind of authority to lead His people.

Then the Lord says, *"...he will become a father to the inhabitants of Jerusalem..."* (see Isa. 22:21). This type of government leader is distinguished from others by having the Father's heart for the people he or she governs. The true bondservant will take on the character, outlook, and desires of his or her Master—the heart of the Father for the people.

# FATHERING SPIRIT

A father does not require a bribe from his children. A father won't oppress or permit injustice to his children.

A father places a higher priority on the welfare of his sons and daughters than on his own life. A father will not steal from the treasury of his children to live in luxury while his children are impoverished. A father will not make empty promises to his distressed children but will take action to alleviate this distress. Fathers don't manipulate their children for their personal benefit. Eliakim was a man who would be a father in the context of God's viewpoint.

I have spoken to and prayed with and for believers who are government leaders all over the world. All of the ones I have met have this sense of a "calling," just as one is "called" to be a pastor. The Lord has uniquely equipped them for the task of governmental leadership. Some of these leaders are obscure; and some occupy the highest positions in government; some have not yet moved into this calling. But all these government leaders have a clear mandate from the Lord.

The Lord said of Eliakim that He would *entrust* him with authority to operate in this new position. He said when Eliakim made decisions, or opened or shut a door, he would have God's backing and support. It is interesting that the Lord didn't say, "As long as you always make every decision correctly, I'll support you."

Decision makers make mistakes. Isaiah 22:22 says, *"Then I will set the key of the house of David on his shoulder, when he opens no one will shut, when he shuts no one will open."* In this verse God was saying, "I trust your motives for making decisions, even when you make mistakes. You have My full support." The Lord would do this because He knew Eliakim's heart was that of a servant of the Most High God and he would do nothing to violate that relationship. The Lord trusted Eliakim to implement His will for the nation of Judah, and He would therefore endorse his decisions. This is a powerful concept.

## THE MANTLE

When the Lord places His mantle (a special grace) on leaders like Eliakim, they will be viewed differently by others. They walk in His favor. We know God's favor is the instrument He uses to bring about change and promotion. They can operate in His wisdom to govern, and as a result, His blessing can flow to their nations because of trustworthy leadership.

The same authority that the Lord delegated to Eliakim belongs to the men and women He has chosen. He will raise up leaders in government for the sake of the people and nations they are to serve. Once again, their personal destinies are secondary. The big picture is much more strategic than personal destiny.

In some nations, the poor are living under oppressive government leaders. Some have become resigned to this oppression as a way of life. However, others are beseeching the God of Heaven for justice and freedom from oppression. This is the reason God is bringing about this change. God hears the cries of these people and He has positioned His bondservants in nations around the globe for just such a time.

# THE HEART OF HUMILITY

Government leadership is an essential element to the culture of every nation. The culture of a nation is like a stool with four legs for support—government, business, education, and ministry. Weakening the legs of the stool makes it unstable. So it is with the culture of any nation. When government leadership is corrupt and does not have the godly characteristics exhibited by men and women like Eliakim, the people are not served and the culture is weakened.

Each of the high-level, influential government leaders I know who are believers has a pastor who serves as a friend and confidential counselor. Some of these leaders sit quietly in church congregations around the world on Sunday mornings. One helps park cars in the church parking lot before Sunday service. They all have a disdain for the culture of corruption that exists and they won't participate in bribery or corruption. Like Eliakim, they have met God's qualifications of humility and servanthood.

I know political leaders who have experienced the "call" to lead their nations. My assessment of them is that they are humble, godly men of great ability and intellect. They speak of their call with a reverence and humility that is unusual for a political leader. In each case, the voice of the Lord has clearly spoken to them about this call and confirmed His Word over and over again through intercessors, pastors, and leaders all over the world. Most of these confirmations came to them in private, out of the eyes of the public. These are men God has appointed to a particular task.

One of these men is a key political leader in Latin America. He told me the Holy Spirit directed him from his country to a conference in Jerusalem with 5,000 people in attendance. He traveled alone, could not understand the language, and sat in the back of the auditorium. At one point, the man leading the conference stopped the meeting, called this leader up to the platform, and under the unction of the Holy Spirit said the Lord was going to "set" him in place as the president of his nation and named his nation.

Another is a man of great ability and intellect who has served his government in very high-level positions. He is a strong believer with a ministry background and the unique calling to lead one of the volatile nations of Africa.

Each of these men told me he would have chosen a different destiny for himself, yet each has a strong sense of God's divine purpose for his life. Each shares the common characteristic of a fathering spirit and a commitment to his destiny.

All of these men are currently serving, or have served, in very high levels of government leadership in their nations. Two have backgrounds as pastors; one came from the business world and one from the military. All four men have said to me, "Why would God choose me for this? I have no qualifications."

If there is one qualification this kind of leader has to have to be a representative of the Lord to the people, it is a father's heart for the people. Each of these men is a man of prayer with a commitment to the ways of God and an overriding sense of responsibility for his nation and the people. Each man has a commitment to the Word and a desire to know God intimately; each has a close personal relationship with his pastor; and each places a high priority on intercession and the intercessor.

## LEADERS WITH THE FATHER'S HEART FOR PEOPLE

I was privileged to spend two days fasting and praying with the president and first lady of an African nation and was left with two very strong impressions of this couple. The first is the godly authority that rested on them. I have never experienced anything like the moment I first saw them come into their living room—their authority was almost tangible. This was clearly supernatural.

The second is the father's and mother's hearts that were so clearly expressed in this couple's prayer for their people. No condescending attitudes were expressed but rather a compassion and love for the people they were called to lead. This must be what the Lord meant when He spoke about Eliakim *"...and he will become a father to the inhabitants of Jerusalem and to the house of Judah"* (Isa. 22:21).

This president had two couples who interceded for him. He covered their expenses out of his personal income, not with government funds. This is integrity on a high level. One of these intercessors told me, "We are in perfect unity and love to pray for the president. At least one of us is praying for the president 24 hours a day.

During the day we pray all day. We pray for his family, for wisdom to lead our nation, for godly counsel for him, and for the favor of God to be on him."

## PUBLIC YET PRIVATE

Leaders like this do not seek platforms to stand up and testify about their call to government leadership in front of their congregations. These Kingdom leaders have made a personal commitment to stand against corruption and bribery, sometimes at the threat of physical harm. They walk in a fear of God that produces high standards of integrity that are required for this kind of leadership.

God's strategy for His Kingdom is to bring His economy to the people. Trusted government leaders who meet His qualifications must be in place for the Lord to open up hidden resources of nations.

Obviously, not all people called to government will lead nations. Some will serve as trusted leaders or counselors, while some will be secretaries or managers. Government people are usually people with influence. For every man or woman summoned to serve God as a government leader, the Lord will send covenant people who ask nothing for themselves, never push personal agendas, refuse the "benefits" that come from these relationships, and do not use this God-given covenant for personal gain. They come only with hearts of servants and intercessors. I will explain what it means to be a friend to this kind of leader in the final chapter.

# What Is God's Opinion on Elected Officials?

The Lord woke me very early one morning with a nation in Central America pressing on my heart. This nation was to have a national election in a few months. As I prayed that morning, the Lord said to me, "My people are distracted by political speeches and personalities. They must come before Me *with one voice* and cry out for *My choice* to lead their nation."

I realized that morning that each time an election or an appointment takes place in a nation, no matter where in the world that may be, God has His choice. He doesn't have a list of backup options if His choice doesn't get elected. He has one choice for each position. His choice represents His will for that nation at that time.

He has a big picture view. He knows what will happen in the future and He always has the benefit of people and the advancement of His Kingdom—not necessarily churches, institutions, or governments—at the forefront of His choices. These things are all elements of His Kingdom, but they cannot be advanced at the expense of the Kingdom.

Yet many times our opinions about candidates are based on newspapers, clever television ads, party affiliation, or candidate speeches. God's opinion needs to be our opinion, and He is willing to share His opinions with us if we take the time to listen. Our priority is to seek Him about elections or appointments in our respective nations.

This seeking has to happen as a Body in each nation. Those who seek God and intercede over their nations and those who take the time to find out God's choices for their leaders will determine the outcome of elections and thereby the history of their nations.

Just as the Lord has destinies for each of us, He has destinies for nations as well (see Matt. 25:32). We seem to be consumed with our personal destinies (the micro viewpoint), and overlook the critical nature of the destiny of nations (the macro viewpoint).

I was recently in an African nation a few months before a national election. I spent some time praying with and for the former vice president of that nation. He was obviously a man with a sincere and deep commitment to God. He told me he had been grieved by recent comments of leading religious leaders of the nation. He said these leaders had been making public comments to the media and their congregations that, "It does not matter who you vote for, only that you participate in the voting process." One of the presidential candidates was involved in witchcraft and had several wives.

God has an opinion on every election and political appointment! He has an opinion about our lives but also about a nation's future. How can we expect the blessing of God on a nation when we just "participate in the process"? We must take the time to find His choices and support His choices! We need to do our due diligence and study the candidates' lives, their affiliations, and their backgrounds and history of decision making. However, it is more important to pray about these matters and find out God's opinion on the matter.

# There Is a New Breed

God's new breed of Kingdom government leaders will be established in every nation by the unified prayer of His saints, not necessarily by political influence alone. We bring this kind of government leader into office by interceding for our nations. We bring in this kind of leadership by crying out to Heaven for His leaders to emerge. The Lord says in Daniel 2:21: *"It is He who changes the times and the epochs; He removes kings and establishes kings...."* Oh Lord, Give us men and women with the heart of Eliakim to lead our nations!

## E N D N O T E S

1. *The Wycliffe Bible Commentary* (Chicago: Moody Bible Institute, 1962), 645.

2. Strong, *A Concise Dictionary of the Words in the Hebrew Bible*, 13.

3. Vine, 1019.

# CHAPTER 11

## *Questions for Consideration*

1. Have you ever considered that there are people around the world who feel God has called them to serve Him in government?

_____

_____

_____

_____

_____

_____

_____

_____

_____

_____

2. Did you know that a righteous and just government is God's way of providing structure to enable people to lead a peaceful life? What is the perversion of God's intent?

_____

_____

_____

_____

_____

_____

_____

_____

3. Have you ever considered that God always has an opinion about who will best fulfill His plan for an elected office? Have you asked Him who He wanted you to vote for?

_____

_____

_____

_____

_____

_____

_____

_____

_____

4. How do you decide who to support during an election?

_____

_____

_____

_____

_____

_____

_____

_____

# CHAPTER 12

## *The Friend of Kings*

*So King Solomon was king over all Israel. And these were his officials: Azariah the son of Zadok, the priest; Elihoreph and Ahijah, the sons of Shisha, scribes; Jehoshaphat the son of Ahilud, the recorder; Benaiah the son of Jehoiada, over the army; Zadok and Abiathar, the priests; Azariah the son of Nathan, over the officers;* **Zabud the son of Nathan, a priest and the king's friend** *(1 Kings 4:1-5 NKJV).*

These verses provide a compelling picture of the Lord's model for leaders. A young Solomon inherited the prestigious role as ruler over the most powerful nation in the Middle East. What is more important, he was ruler over a people set apart by God as His own. In the third chapter of First Kings, Solomon told the Lord he was ill-equipped to lead His people. After he stated his case to the Lord,

Solomon asked Him for a special impartation of wisdom and an understanding heart to judge God's people.

Solomon's request pleased the Lord so much that He equipped Solomon with even more than he asked for! Therefore, at least in his early years, Solomon was a leader with unparalleled wisdom and insight. He was given this gift from the Lord because he valued wisdom and understanding more than great riches—a reminder for the leaders of today.

In this text we are learning about the formal "cabinet" of advisors who surrounded the new king. These men helped Solomon administer and lead the great nation of Israel. One of the basic principles of leadership is to surround oneself with wise counselors. Apparently Solomon was not a micromanager who wanted to control every detail of the administration of the Kingdom of Israel. He relied on able, loyal, proven men to execute the details of the strategies of their king. However, one name and role in the "cabinet" stands out from the rest: *"Zabud the son of Nathan, **a priest and the king's friend.**"*

Did Solomon actually give cabinet status to a "friend"? The answer is yes, he did. However, Solomon had a precedent to follow. His father, King David, one of the greatest leaders in history and certainly of Israel, established this precedent. *"Ahithophel was counselor to the king; and Hushai the Archite **was the king's friend"*** (1 Chron. 27:33).

## ISOLATION, LONELINESS, AND CRITICISM

Leaders often experience a strong sense of isolation, loneliness, and criticism. The leader can be president of a bank, principal of a school, pastor of a church, a leader of a business or a department, or the leader of the government of a nation. Leadership is generally accompanied by these three elements in varying degrees, depending on the level of leadership.

Isolation accompanies leadership because no matter how inclusive the leadership style is, the leader is ultimately responsible for the results. Leaders are lonely because the higher the level of leadership, the more likely it is that others will try to use their relationship for "favors."

In this case, leaders become suspicious and careful about friendships. Most leaders learn to tolerate the element of criticism. However, criticism of leadership sometimes comes in the form of an assault on character. This can be difficult for anyone to endure.

When you are out front as a leader, you are constantly subject to other people's opinions on how you should do things. When things are going well, the opinionated often view it as "success in spite of leadership." When things are not going well, often it is viewed as a direct result of failed leadership. (A study of the Book of Zechariah reveals these concepts in the lives of two of God's appointed leaders, Joshua the priest and Zerubbabel the governor.)

Though there may be some truth to both types of criticisms, the Lord is showing us an overriding issue in these verses—the leader's need for a friend.

Solomon operated with a supernatural wisdom that few have known, yet he appointed this man Zabud to the cabinet to be his friend. Why was this man Zabud appointed to such an unusual position? What were his qualifications? How did he carry out his duties as a "friend"?

## The Koheen

God is giving us a picture of a man who was chosen to be among the leaders of Israel, whose sole purpose was to "associate with, as a friend" and to be a *koheen* or "confidential advisor of the king."[1] Even the Hebrew name *Zabud* means "to endure."[2] I believe we are getting a picture of a man who had a faithful, enduring friendship with the King.

We don't know much about Zabud. Most likely his work was done in private. Many Bible scholars say that Zabud was not the son of Nathan, the priest and prophet of David's day, but of another Nathan. He was a "layman" and a "principal officer," not a professional priest. However, Zabud was a man of priestly character who served as one of Solomon's closest advisors.

His role was to listen, be a loyal friend, and give godly counsel to God's appointed leader. How many leaders long for this kind of man or woman in their lives? What does this role of a *koheen* look like today? How does one serve leaders in this kind of role?

## Leaders Need a Koheen

God is the One who sets people in positions of authority. Daniel 2:21 says, *"It is He who changes the times and the epochs; He removes kings and establishes kings...."* We live in a day when He is removing leaders and establishing His leaders. In almost every nation, God seems to be moving in the area of leadership. Leadership organizations are cropping up everywhere. Some teach God's principles for leadership and some are teaching the principles of the world.

As mentioned, I have had the privilege of knowing several godly political leaders of other nations. Though the needs of each nation may be different, the personal needs of these leaders remain the same. Each of these godly men and women need someone to counter the isolation, loneliness, and criticism with simple friendship and godly counsel.

We must recognize that being a friend to a leader, no matter what kind of leader, is a sacred position. God does not want His leaders to live a life of isolation, loneliness, and criticism. Our God believes in the sanctity of relationships, and the relationship of a friend to a leader is a high calling. What does the unique role of the "friend of a king" look like in today's world? Is it as relevant today as it was in Solomon's day?

## DEFINING THE ROLE OF A FRIEND

- **Taking Sides**—A koheen, or "confidential advisor," does not take sides against his or her friend. The friend of a leader cannot take sides, either in his thought life or in conversation with others, against the one he or she stands alongside. This kind of friend must remain loyal and faithful. This does not mean that when the leader is operating in immorality or unrighteousness that the friend keeps silent. To do so would be a violation of a sacred holy trust. Proverbs 27:6 says, *"Faithful are the wounds of a friend...."* This kind of "wound" or correction can be received because the source can be trusted to have the best interest of the leader at heart. This "wound of correction" may not always be received, but it must always be given.

- **Jealousy**—The position of a friend often provokes jealousy on the part of others. It is important to recognize a spiritual dynamic is taking place. One of the basic tactics of the devil is to divide and conquer. He wants to divide or separate the leader from godly counsel and friendships. This produces isolation because spiritual strength is derived from unity. Once the enemy isolates, he will conquer by discrediting or discouraging God's leaders. God's appointed leaders pose the real threat to the enemy's kingdom of darkness. People will often try to get access to the leader through the friend. Others also will try to undermine the role of a friend in the life of the "king" by subtle personal attacks or raising questions of motive. Daniel experienced this in the court of the Persian king. The jealousy of the other advisors led to Daniel's night in the lion's den. The position of a friend will always come under some kind of attack. When God gives this position of influence, the defense against the attack also belongs to Him. We cannot defend what does not belong to us. The Lord is able to defend His gifts, His favor, and His purposes.

- **Personal Gain**—The influence that comes with being a friend to leaders is God-given. He gives this influence not for the personal advancement of the friend but for the sake of the leader. The friend serves as a conduit for the Lord to the leader. A friend can say what others cannot say. A friend will hear what others will never hear. The moment the friend considers using this God-given position for personal gain, the conduit is broken and a holy trust has been violated. When the conduit from the Lord is broken because of selfish ambition or motives, the favor of God also is gone. In a short time, the friend's influence is over. Jesus is our example. He came to earth from the right hand of the Father with one purpose: to influence the destiny of the lives of all humanity. He was offered much personal gain if He would modify His purpose. Thanks be to God, Jesus chose to stay the course. If God places you in this position, expect nothing but to serve as a friend. Do not use your position for personal enrichment or personal gain or your influence will end. The friend has an unusual status that is distinguished from all others in that he or she asks for nothing for himself or herself and comes only to serve in this role as friend.

- **Trust**—I have a friend who serves in the position of friend to many political leaders in Africa. Years ago he was a young associate pastor when he began praying for the leader of his nation. At the time, a leader had ruled his nation for many years as an atheist, Marxist dictator. My friend prayed every day, two hours a day, for ten years for this man. I asked him what he prayed for every day for two hours. He said, "I prayed for his family, his children, his protection, the wisdom of God to lead our nation, and his salvation and the salvation of his family." He never once prayed for an audience with the man, nor did he pray for his removal from office.

When communism fell, this leader's financial base was gone as well. To his credit, the dictator called for the first free elections in the nation's history. During one of those times of prayer, the Lord gave my friend a word for this leader. My pastor friend was an obscure man with no influence to deliver God's message to a man surrounded by soldiers carrying AK-47s. Yet within 24 hours he found himself in a room of the presidential palace alone with this leader to deliver God's word. The word was that he would lose the election. If he did not contest the election, God would establish him again as the leader and he would lead in righteousness. Everything happened just as the Lord said it would, and the leader received Christ during the process.

Why would God choose my friend rather than another to deliver His message? Why would God also use my friend to bring this leader to Christ? The answer is that this pastor could be trusted. He could be trusted because he was faithful in his prayer life to speak to the Father about this leader when others had opinions about his leadership. He called this man's name to the attention of the throne of Heaven while no one was looking, with no personal expectations or ambitions. He became this leader's friend and eventually his pastor. Because he will take nothing for his friendship, he is a man this leader can trust. More importantly, he is a man God can trust with His kind of influence.

- **Sanctity of Conversation**—Zabud may have listened to things that others never heard. To remain in this critical role as a friend who advised, he had to do more listening than talking. When Zabud was tempted to tell others about the personal things Solomon shared, he must have listened to another voice whispering the words of loyalty, covenant, and honor. A friend never shares the intimacy of private conversations and never allows others to manipulate them into doing so. Things spoken in private remain private and become matters for prayer.

## WHO INFLUENCES THE INFLUENCERS?

Influence is an instrument of leadership. Leaders, whether they are in the political, ministerial, or business worlds, wield great influence. They understand the nature and use of this mystical dynamic called influence. Some use it as a weapon against others. Some use influence to further their personal agendas.

God is bringing to the fore His kind of leader around the world. This is a move of God in our day. He will empower these leaders with His favor and His anointing to influence decisions that will affect God's first love—people. Whom will God use to influence these influencers? It may be a man or woman like you.

## ENDNOTES

1. James Strong, S.T.D., LL.D., *A Concise Dictionary of the Words in the Hebrew Bible* (Madison, NJ: Strong, 1890), 54.

2. Ibid, 34.

# CHAPTER 12

## *Questions for Consideration*

1. Have you ever considered that leaders, particularly high level leaders, need friends they can talk to confidentially?

_____

_____

_____

_____

_____

2. What do you think would be a few characteristics of this kind of friend?

_____

_____

_____

3. Do you think this kind of friend should not ask for personal favors or benefits?

_____

_____

_____

_____

_____

_____

_____

_____

_____

4. Could you qualify as the friend of a leader? Why or why not?

_____

_____

_____

_____

_____

_____

_____

_____

_____

5. Have you ever violated a confidentiality of friendship?

_____

_____

_____

_____

_____

_____

_____

_____

_____

_____

# About Paul L. Cuny

Paul Cuny is the founder and president of Market-Place Leadership International, a ministry preparing leaders and professionals on several continents with the Kingdom principles necessary to excel in our rapidly changing world. Paul's background of serving God in the business world as an entrepreneur and business owner has equipped him to speak from a unique platform. He is an ordained minister with a call to teach the biblical principals of the Economy of the Kingdom to marketplace people around the world.

He had a paradigm shift in the mid-90s when the Lord spoke two things that would define the rest of his life: "You will change the economies of nations!" and "I will use you to speak to leaders of nations on My behalf." Since that time, Paul has held MarketPlace Leadership Conferences in Central America, South America, Africa, and the United States to teach marketplace people how to succeed through the practical application of the biblical principles of the Kingdom of God in business.

Paul has ministered to political leaders from several continents. He has prayed with and served as a counselor to high-level political leaders from a number of nations, including a private time of prayer and fasting with the president and first lady of an African nation.

Paul Cuny is an international conference and church speaker who speaks on biblical leadership and the economic principles of the Kingdom of God in professional life. He has published numerous articles on leadership and the practical workings of the Economy of the Kingdom. He serves as counselor and consultant to government and business leaders, as well as serving as a board member on two international ministries. Paul Cuny is a graduate of Florida State University and resides in Jacksonville, Florida.

# *Contact Information*

To contact the author to speak at your conference, marketplace gathering, or church, please write to:

PAUL L. CUNY

MarketPlace Leadership International

email: paul@marketplaceleadership.com

www.marketplaceleadership.com

blog site: www.themarketplacejournal.com

# IN THE RIGHT HANDS, THIS BOOK WILL CHANGE LIVES!

Most of the people who need this message will not be looking for this book. To change their lives, you need to put a copy of this book in their hands.

> *But others (seeds) fell into good ground, and brought forth fruit, some a hundred-fold, some sixty-fold, some thirty-fold* (Matthew 13:8).

Our ministry is constantly seeking methods to find the good ground, the people who need this anointed message to change their lives. Will you help us reach these people?

> *Remember this—a farmer who plants only a few seeds will get a small crop. But the one who plants generously will get a generous crop* (2 Corinthians 9:6).

**EXTEND THIS MINISTRY BY SOWING
3 BOOKS, 5 BOOKS, 10 BOOKS, OR MORE TODAY,
AND BECOME A LIFE CHANGER!**

Thank you,

Don Nori Sr., Publisher
Destiny Image
Since 1982